When
Your
Child
Needs
You

When Your Child Needs You

You

A Parents' Guide through the Early Years

ELEANOR WEISBERGER

ADLER&ADLER

Published in the United States in 1987
by
Adler & Adler, Publishers, Inc.
4550 Montgomery Avenue
Bethesda, Maryland 20814

Library of Congress
Cataloging-in-Publication Data

Weisberger, Eleanor.
When your child needs you.

Includes index.
1. Child rearing. 2. Parent and child. 3.
Child psychology. I. Title.
HQ769.W429 1987 649'.1 86-14197
ISBN 0-917561-31-7
ISBN 0-917561-33-3 (pbk.)

Printed in the United States of America

For David, the compleat pediatrician

CONTENTS

INTRODUCTION

*I*N 1975 I wrote a book entitled *Your Young Child and You* with the intention of helping parents understand the child's growing-up problems in years one through five. The book was based on my many years of experience working in a children's clinic as a child therapist. The topics I featured, such as separation, toilet training, sex education, and hospitalization, attracted a sizable readership because those rearing young children were finding that early childhood was not the serene time they had envisioned—either for children or their parents. The book was about the raising of children, not as a dream fulfillment, but as it really happens in daily life.

Since the publication of my last book, children have not changed; their needs remain the same. But in the past decade, society has changed—or at least half of it has. In the early seventies it was assumed that the majority of mothers of preschool-age children were at home and that the major share of child rearing was done by them. Today, however, more than half of the mothers of children under five are working outside the home, and good care for infants and preschoolers has become a large issue.

Child-care professionals wishing to help working parents cope with this issue have recommended group care of various kinds. Yet recently some professionals in the field have been questioning what this type of care means in the lives of young children. Indeed, the economic pressures of the 1980s often determine the choices of many working parents, and no one wants to inflict guilt on mothers, in particular, who are out in the work force in great numbers. Everyone devoted to the care of children wants to help. But mothers themselves are finding that there isn't time to "do it all," and they are concerned about the long-term effects leaving their children in the care of others will have on them.

I see many parents of young children in my practice and I am saddened by the view of some that they have no alternative but to leave their young children in someone else's care. They are missing out on the basic attachment that starts to happen the minute they become responsible for fulfilling their babies' needs. As they respond to baby, baby responds to them, and a pattern of love develops that gradually enables parents to have influence over their children's lives.

The importance of this early attachment of parent and child was once an assumption so widespread in this country it barely required explication. The nuclear family was the basic element in society. In fact, I opened my first book with a chapter on how to toilet train, since infancy was a period I felt all agreed was a time requiring individual care and nothing need be said about it. This is no longer the case and can no longer be taken for granted.

This book is an effort to fill in the gaps in the recent literature on child rearing—which tends to support what *is happening* rather than what *should be happening* for the healthy development of the young—and have parents look at the whole picture. The growth of the child-care industry developed as a response to the needs of adults, not of children. It did not come about because people were looking for a new, more communal way to raise their young. It seemed a necessary service since mothers were, in increasing numbers, away from home. The part of the child-rearing picture that is missing for those parents weighing options is, to my mind, the need of all young children for individual care by someone who loves them. Denying that this need is a reality *too* in today's muddled world of colliding priorities does not offer parents the right to make the best choice for their children.

When Your Child Needs You: A Parents' Guide through the Early Years is addressed to all parents, but will be particularly helpful, I think, to those mothers caught among their own needs, the needs of their families, and those of their children. It is both a description and a prescription. It describes how children develop and then suggests ways for the mother, father, or caretaker to help children become their better selves. The book encourages mothers who have a choice to stay home to do so. It is helpful as well to the working mother in that it gives suggestions about how to help children through the difficulties of separation that work entails. Parents can, therefore, use the information according to their own family situation. Several of the "how to" chapters of my earlier book are revised and updated here, but the text has been expanded to describe in greater detail how the infant and toddler think. If we understand children's incomplete and very narrow view of things and listen to what they are telling us—first in actions, then in words—I think we can function more effectively in our child rearing. And the "how to's" are useful in a commonsense way because they rest on what we know about the normal ups and downs of early childhood.

For those fathers who stay home either to take over the care of the children or pitch in while mother is away, the recommendations in this book hold equally for them. Chapter Twelve discusses the father's role in the family. Many more fathers are helping out than ever before, so that the work is shared.

Throughout the text, I have referred to the caretaking parent as "she" and the child as "he," because to do otherwise in English is impossibly awkward. And the more the father or caretaker substitute is involved, the more he needs to know what mother knows, so when father or caretaker is doing primary care, substitute "father" or "caretaker" for "mother." This makes the book simpler to read.

It should prove some comfort for women who face the dilemma of working and rearing a baby to know that the child's elemental need for closeness lessens as he gets older. The children slowly pull away and make their own friends, only touching base when the need arises. Other people become important to them, adding new influences to a developing personality. This should encourage all those who have been told "they can do it all," only to find it is not possible. Maybe we should revise the slogan to read: "You can do it all—but not simultaneously, not at the same time." Given the lengthened life expectancy women have today, the time spent with little ones in their early years is not all that long a time.

The goal of all caretakers is to raise a potentially mature being. But the baby needs a tie to someone dear if this potential is to unfold. Parenthood is a commitment to children, and it is never too soon to restate the importance of this commitment in the early years of child development. My hope is that this book will encourage parents to reap the positive pleasures of being able to fulfill their children's needs and in an indirect but real way fulfill themselves.

1.
The Mother's Dilemma

*T*HERE are many truths in child rearing. We know that children need love but also discipline, that they need indulgence but also limits. We know that good kids come from all sorts of families—strict, casual, and in-between. We have learned a lot about child development and about what can go wrong in the child's early years. As concerned parents, we read widely and try to pull together information that seems to fit our particular family situation. On the whole, there is a lot of soul searching on the part of American parents who want the best for their children.

One of the important truths, which was once assumed almost universally, is that what happens in a child's early years makes a significant difference in later life. This underlies much of our anxiety. If things that happen to the under-five-year-old are so important to his future well-being, then we all feel we must try our best to "do it right" in the first years.

Trying to do it right is what makes parents so eager to understand children and is what accounts for the books and articles devoted to constructive parenting. In the past decade, trying to do it right has taken on a new dimension because the traditional role of mothers, who are, according to statistics, still the primary caretakers of their children, has changed.

The viewpoints of the mothers who are staying home to care for the under-fives and those working away from home differ enormously. Each group tends to justify whatever path it has chosen. While many mothers who are home feel that what they provide is constant, and therefore better, care for their children, many working mothers maintain that they are better mothers because of the break in schedule. They feel their enjoyment of their work makes for more family contentment, not less. It is certainly true that each of us has a human tendency to be subjective about ourselves and objective toward others. And we are inclined to defend the merits of our choice when challenged by others who think differently. Rearing children is not an easy matter in any event, for both mothers who stay home and mothers employed outside the home; the goal for each is a similar one—to raise healthy, well-adjusted children. Both groups of mothers are indeed working hard. And each, in her own way, is paying a price for her choice.

The Mother on the Job

The mother on the job has the problem of the work place not acknowledging her "mother life." She may find that her employer is not interested in her child's emotional upsets, his illnesses, or her fatigue in juggling the many demands on her time. Further, she recognizes her child's need for continuity and love and wants someone to give the full-time loving care she can only give intermittently. The business world's emphasis is on personal achievement and operates on principles other than affection and loyalty. Jobs value competency, competitiveness, and being in control. Despite a few isolated exam-

ples of flextime, working mothers with young children
have to bend to the demands of the work place. The job
is considered central by both employer and employee;
whatever a mother does for her child is done by her
outside of working hours.

The different hats she wears as she goes from one
profession to another do not rest easy on the working
mother's head. What is hardest for the mother working
full time away from home is not being with her child
enough. As I see these mothers in my practice, I can see
how torn they are by the many claims on their time.
When the children themselves are able to voice feelings,
mothers often hear a refrain that is no fun to listen to.

"Mom," said a three-and-a-half-year-old to her mother
as they approached the day-care center, "is it against the
law for you to stay home?"

A four-year-old, on his way to his sitter for the day,
scribbled on a picture he had just drawn.

His mother asked, "Why did you mess up your picture?"

"That wasn't a picture," he snapped. "That was a message!"

This was a mother who had worked through her
child's infancy and preschool years. His behavior in nursery school, to which he was taken by his sitter, had
made this mother look into the message he was sending.
She was concerned, when she consulted me, about his
wild temper tantrums and general unfocused destruc-
tiveness. One didn't have to be extraordinarily percep-
tive to see anger that was way out of control. When I
paid a home visit, he threw a golf ball at my head, nar-
rowly missing me, but making his point even more force-
fully. He didn't want to share his time with his mother
with *anyone*.

Another mother who has an eighteen-month-old
daughter in day care told me she cannot bear to see her
little girl's unhappiness when she leaves her at the cen-

ter. The child becomes withdrawn and mute when she is left, therefore mother, too, is silent and withdrawn when they part. The connection to her child, which this mother values, is too painful to encourage because she does not want to hear her child's distress. No talk goes on between them. As a mother who has no choice but to work, she turns away. Each faces her world alone.

One working mother who consulted me about her three-year-old who was not talking at all at the sitter's was astonished to hear her child say to me as they left my office, "Tell Mommy 'tay home."

This kind of story is heard in my office more and more frequently these days, and it does not make the working women I see feel good about their double responsibilities. A working mother has to make arrangements for her child if she is to work, and she tries hard to make good provision for her child's care. To hear from the children themselves that this is an arrangement that makes them unhappy adds anxiety and more concern to an already difficult situation. To learn further that children up to three may not be served well in group care despite good planning can be devastating to the working mother. The attachment issue before the age of three (see Chapter Two) is paramount in the life of a child, and acknowledging the importance of the mother-child tie in the early years only makes her employment more of a stress than ever. When one is working hard to support children, it is not so sweet to hear that they may be shortchanged emotionally by the very work that provides for them.

Those who advocate group care for young children are generally upbeat in their reporting to parents. They see such care as being better for young children. They describe the children in day-care centers as being made more independent by virtue of the separation from their mothers, and they claim most of their charges wave bye-bye with a big smile when Mommy leaves. They contrast this behavior with the clinginess a mother at home often faces when she leaves a toddler at nursery school for the first time. "He stops crying the moment you leave," is frequently heard. The inference here is that the mother has a problem leaving her child and the child can handle separation well if there is no interference from Mom.

To confuse mothers even further, not all children in day care show separation feelings in the way child development professionals have come to recognize. Some children *do* wave bye-bye; others cry when mothers leave. Some suck their thumbs or look forlorn; others dance off without a backward glance. How are we to read these? Are they emotional statements of any significance? Is it normal for children to go happily to anyone they don't know? Do we get what we see?

In addition to this confusion there is also the problem of what substitute caretakers tell us. Can we trust their reports? Are they not committed to making things work regardless of what they see? Don't they want to spare the working mother anxiety?

So who is right and who is wrong? Are a child's separation feelings normal? What are mothers, those working outside the home and those not, to believe? The other side of the coin—mothers at home—also brings doubt and confusion.

The Mother at Home

Mothers who are staying home with their preschoolers are faced with difficulties, too. They are challenged by those who want to see women emancipated from the home, and they may, in fact, question whether being home with young children is necessary for their development. Is the attachment between mother and child they have read about really necessary? If being home is so good for the children, why is it so difficult for the parents who are doing the raising?

The status in the community of the mother-at-home is generally at a fairly low ebb today.

"What do *you* do?" is asked of her when she is out. The questioner often doesn't mean taking care of a child. He or she means what paid, purposeful work do you do that society values? When she answers that she is a housewife raising children, it is as though she turns into a nonperson. The response is "Oh," as the questioner turns away.

There is the assumption, very much recognized by the mother at home, that she must be a person without goals and without ambition. An inference hangs over her head that she lacks ability and is not capable of work more demanding than changing diapers. With all the hype today about women's freedom to choose careers, there is a very clear put-down of those doing old-fashioned women's work—caring for children.

The proposition that this might be a thoughtful and well-considered choice is foreign to much current opinion. If in the old days it took courage to step outside the confines of the home to pursue a career, now it takes courage to stay home. The idea that a mother may feel she is making a contribution to the life of a child seems to have been lost by a good number of women in this difficult decade of change.

Doubts and Decisions

Yet both groups want the best for their children. The mother on the job is looking for a substitute for herself who will offer the nurturing and care she cannot give except in an intermittent sense—at the beginning or end of a long day. Such caretakers are not easy to find, and many who offer child care are not of the caliber mothers feel good about.

One mother in search of a caretaker put an ad in the paper for a motherly, intelligent, loving person, compassionate and nurturing. She wanted the woman to speak

English well since her child would be learning to talk in her presence. After a month of interviews, it dawned on her that there was only one person who fit the requirements.

"Who was it?" I asked.

"Me," she said.

This is a particularly hard realization for the mother who, for economic or career reasons, feels she has no choice but to work. So the quest for nannies and special people goes on. Some mothers I know are leaving high-paying jobs and significant careers to be the primary caregivers of their children. Several who had worked through the early years of the first child are now staying home with the second. Books are now being published by women with this point of view. They reason that despite the loss of income, position, and tenure, their decision is a good one for their families, even though they will pay a price if they decide to reenter the job market later.

This doesn't mean the decision is an easy one. For a woman who is accustomed to having a lot of liberty, it is an enormous change. Unless she makes arrangements for her child to be cared for when she goes away, she is totally and absolutely stuck in the home.

Before she became a mother and decided to stay home, a woman could exert control over many things in her life. She could take pleasure in being competent at a job or profession. She got paid for her work—there was concrete recognition of her worth. There were coffee breaks, status, money for a wardrobe and she got to go home at the end of a day. This changes radically with the advent of the newborn. Someone else's needs come first. This is an adjustment of some proportion. The new mother's feelings of incompetence compound matters because nobody can be experienced before one experiences the experience.

"I felt," said one mother of her mothering, "as if I'd been sent to the Olympics when I'd never been on a ski slope before."

Not yet knowing how to do what needs doing and the insult of being put down by peers all contribute to the downcast feelings young mothers are experiencing. The fact that so many mothers are not at home today also contributes to the feeling of isolation. Mothers at home lack the companionship of their peers.

In addition, the newcomer for whom this is being done doesn't bring immediate satisfaction. While the joys of motherhood may still be extolled in song and story (and belittled everywhere else), everyone misses an exchange with a person of some intelligence.

"I felt my intellectual level had peaked at 7:30 in the morning," said one mother.

After a stretch of colic or of night waking, of a long winter of sniffles and snowpants, doubts about the pleasures of mothering can arise even after one has made the decision to raise one's child oneself. A mother of two, a toddler and a new infant, commented to me that she rarely had time for the quality time child-care books talk about. She was busy all day long, and at the end of a day, she could barely rouse herself to read the third story her toddler demanded. "Maybe if I had a job," she said, "I'd come home and pay better attention. Then I could read stories, play with them, and enjoy them more."

Quantity Time

This reflects a common confusion about quality time. I think the phrase came into being because mothers who were away working wanted to feel that the small quantity of time they had with their children was special. There was a fun and games idea in it as if to make up for their absence. And if stimulating and cognitive features were introduced in addition, they had the feeling they were enriching their children's lives.

8

No one can really argue about this—and certainly not with mothers who miss their children and want to spend time with them that's special at the end of a day. But it is not a central need of children in the early years.

What is needed in the early years is quantity time. The premise of the following chapters is that motherhood is not a given. Mothering is an ongoing process—one that occurs over the course of much time spent with a child —through infancy, the terrible twos, toilet training, and separations, small and large. When most mothers were home with young children, little thought was given to the importance of this because it was built into the system. Now there is a need to explain the importance of the bond that slowly develops between mother and child as she fulfills his needs. And this early period of child development requires special attention today because other options are now available that were not always open to women in the past. Therefore, the following chapters will enable those who have a choice about whether to work or not in their child's early years to really understand what their choice can mean to a child. For those who have no choice but to work, finding the right person as a substitute will be the important issue. Fathers, too, can make a difference in the lives of their children when this need is understood. But rarely, unless they are at home raising the children (some few do), are they as significant in the early years as are mothers.

2.

Attachment in the Early Years

No ONE ever interviewed a baby. He can't talk. He can't describe his needs. We are guessing about him much of the time.

Close observations of him by psychologists and pediatricians recently have increased, however, and we have learned some new things.

1. He can see at birth.

2. He prefers a human face to any other object from the start.

3. His smile is genuine (any grandmother could have told you it wasn't gas but no one was listening back then).

Today we are recognizing that he has more antennae out than we ever thought, and this new knowledge has spurred a tremendous interest in his beginnings. Birth centers, husbands helping during delivery, immediate holding after birth—all have contributed to this almost reverential respect for the miracle of life.

But bonding, as important as it is, is to raising a child as the wedding is to a marriage. It's only the beginning. And the first, second, and third years, yes, even the fourth, fifth, and sixth years of life are critical for what happens later, for these years are a child's emotional foundation.

There are those who see mothering as an innate instinct that will take care of things without effort or reflection. This may be so in the animal world, but it is certainly not true of human beings. For there are ways and then there are ways of caring for a baby. For baby to become the best he can be, a tie needs to be forged between the mother and child at the beginning. Baby is incomplete at first—he can do nothing for himself to ensure his survival, and while he has the capability for growth, his best self does not evolve without the continuous presence of a loved partner. Baby in a real sense is only a potential person who grows into himself by the care he is given. The kind of care makes a significant difference. It's a little like the development of a negative in photography; the proper solution is necessary.

Making the Connection

To help raise a mature person from the tiny bundle you start with takes a great deal more than good physical care. Physical development may be a fairly maturational process but there is nothing automatic about a child's emotional, intellectual, or ethical development. These come gradually in small incremental steps and over time. Tracing these steps, we see that an infant starts life by wanting what he wants when he wants it. In the beginning his own needs come first and it is the way in which these needs are met that makes a significant difference in his personality later on. Intelligence, language, the development of character—all these unfold over the love attachment that builds. They are embedded in the child in the thousands of interactions that go on daily between parent and child. The teaching that is offered by parents in this fashion is indirect. It comes in the way we relate to him and in our response to his needs. He learns to be giving because he's been given. Eventually he can be trusted because we have been trustworthy. This constancy above anything else we do makes him educable to our values—an important issue in today's troubled times.

We know all this about infants from the tragic accidents of life that have been reported in the psychological literature from all over the world. In these reports of children separated from parents by war or other natural disasters, one is able to see what is missing in their emotional lives. And in the direct treatment of children by professionals like myself and others, we have also had confirmatory evidence about the need for the on-scene love tie for babies. Many children we therapists see in our offices today have not suffered the big disasters mentioned above but rather small ones—divorce and loss of a parent at an early time—also, daily separation in group day-care programs in infancy and the preschool years. We have seen that even the best of those programs do not suffice when it comes to the emotional needs of babies and toddlers. For the prime need of the baby and preschooler is for one (or two) people who value him above all else and who give him time. Sharing even the finest environment with so many others in a group can water him down as a person. Love is an exclusive emotion and people who care for a baby are not interchangeable for him. You see this as you as a mother become a full-time caregiver. It becomes clear to you how much your baby needs you. And it is in your caring that you awaken his emotional life.

First Achievements

What does baby learn in his first year of life?
1. He learns to know his mother.
2. He learns to love his mother.

3. He learns to miss his mother when she leaves.

This is no small achievement for an infant. He is becoming attached to a person who, by the very act of her caretaking, locks him in to her. It makes how she views things very persuasive for him. The sense of a family with its own unique continuity begins.

This doesn't mean a baby *thinks* as we do, however. Up to the age of five or six months a baby thinks an object has disappeared forever when he can't see it. Experiments with babies show that they stop looking when a ball is put behind a pillow and hidden from their view. Later, at seven or eight months, they keep looking for the ball. Baby now knows the ball exists even if he can't see it—and that you, who have been constantly there for him, still exist, even when you leave. You are now a being he can retain in his mind. The repeated experiences he has in your being there over time has helped fix you in his thinking as "real."

This is an important intellectual step for him. He is beginning to absorb the facts about a real world. But now that he values you so much, he is easily upset when you go away. Toward the end of his first year, he often screams at the sight of an unfamiliar face. Feel complimented. This, too, is progress. For he is becoming discriminating and can now distinguish his own person from any other. His attachment to you can be seen in the anguish he exhibits when you leave and his fright at the sight of a "not mother" face. Emotions are surfacing now because he is becoming more of a person.

The baby who is so friendly and goes to anyone (many day-care workers point with pride to such a baby) is not likely to do this. He hasn't locked in his own person enough for separation to matter much to him. He doesn't care enough to be upset. That's a worry for all of us, both parents and professionals, because feelings about separation are normal. They stem from being connected to others and attest to the strength of emotional commitment.

The Mother-Child Unit

Nature actually has a neat system for helping mothers understand their infants' behavior. As you care for a baby, you are getting hooked. With the gurgling, smiles, and face brightening you see, you are falling in love with your own baby. The emotional satisfaction you receive is almost impossible to put into words without sounding sappy.

As baby cries, you respond. Baby is appeased; you are delighted. Slowly you begin to catch on to what he is asking for. You feel more competent as you are able to decipher his signals. You have become the great tension reliever, feeder, diaper changer, hurt soother, cuddler, burper, path clearer, and many other things you had never anticipated. What you are doing in the first year, in general, is responding to him. You are enjoying your child's babyhood and meeting his needs as he is feeling them. The mother-child unit begins to form. Just as your responsiveness supports his development, so his responsiveness turns you into a mother. The taking care promotes the caring.

On the other hand, you are never free for a moment. How can one baby take up so much time? The experienced mother of many children will say they *all* take up *all* time no matter how few or how many you have.

In the first year your baby has learned to know you. And now, when he does, he wants only you. So you are really caught. Now when baby cries, you hurt. He has become more important than you ever anticipated. Yet he can make you so mad you sometimes want to wring his little neck. He wails; he smells; he teethes; he's prone to stuffy noses and other ailments. To make it harder, most of the time you have to guess about what will please him because he can't tell you. What sustains you is the tie that you now feel.

It is this tie that enables you to put up with the endless cycle of care—loss of sleep, fatigue. Observers of a mother often don't see that she is doing much of *anything*, but if they look closely, they see she is busy all the time: responding, clearing away things that upset her baby. Now, by virtue of these many small interchanges a mother has with her infant, what she is really doing is making a world that is good for him. This solidifies baby's ability to face that world and is an important step in his future ability to learn. We know we all learn better when our relationship with our teachers is good rather than poor. This simple idea begins in the cradle. Only as we are older can we separate the material to be learned from the giver. So what we do with a baby to help him learn later in life is to provide the kind of security that makes him want to learn, that enables him to be interested in what's out there because his needs have been met by a loving person. He isn't spending all his energy trying to meet his own needs or in denying he has any —the false independence some toddlers exhibit. In effect we are helping to develop a mind. This effort enables us later to instruct that mind.

Small Changes: Six to Twelve Months

In the second half of the first year, you see small changes. Your child becomes restless when he is held; he squirms when you diaper him. He is more interested in things; he examines objects with an intensity he didn't show before. He wants to do more for himself—grasping, sitting, pulling himself up, crying, standing. Even at this early age you encourage his independence by allowing him to do whatever he can for himself, even to feeding himself in the high chair. From being the all-important provider of the first six months, you become the allower and encourager of the second six months and indeed of the year that follows. You will recognize signs of his losing interest in breast or bottle somewhere toward the end of the first year. He will push the nipple out of his mouth, turn away. He is giving you the signal that he is ready to move on to greener pastures. Your allowing him to move to a cup gradually reflects your ability to understand what he is telling you by his behavior. His pride in learning to do new things in a more grown-up way is an early building block in self-esteem.

Big Changes: The Second Year

The second year is the year of big change.

Your child is not only walking but talking; furthermore, he understands much more than he can say. Maturation has gone swiftly, and he's no longer a baby. A toddler is more like it. He may still look like a baby to you because you are so close to him, but it helps that you recognize that he's growing up. He is now ready for a different kind of interaction with you. The responsive cycle you've shared with him in his first year and even the encouragement of the last months of that year make way for your adapting to more changes going on in him.

This is a person with so much energy that you wonder why you ever wished him out of the playpen. He has the ability to go off on his own and is fascinated by everything around him—especially electric outlets. What he hasn't got much of is steering ability. You find you will be doing most of the piloting with your "yesses" and "nos." Your house may start to look like the last day of a garage sale as treasured objects disappear into a back closet. Retreating temporarily in this fashion makes sense because he doesn't have much ability to control his impulses. You find you have to say "no" a lot at this age, because he's into everything. What aggravates you is the mischievous provocation of some of his behavior. He can look you squarely in the face as he deliberately and carefully does what you have expressly forbidden. What he's

16

doing is trying you out, finding where the limits are. He's also enjoying his new abilities and learning something about what he, as a separate person from you, is able to do. Or not do.

It's a good step in his development. Now he is active on his own behalf and his curiosity brings him knowledge (albeit of a limited sort) as he maneuvers himself into all kinds of predicaments.

Knowing what to overlook at this time is valuable. There are advantages to letting some things pass when they are not important. It lets you keep your ammunition for what really counts and reduces the number of conflicts. Doing so makes for greater emotional tranquility and a better general climate. Here allowable alternatives make sense. Pots, pans, and sturdy toys are useful, since a toddler is busy testing, biting, and banging. Clay, Play-doh, and water are helpful because he enjoys making messes. Don't worry about clean-ups at this time; he's still too young for these. Just set yourself up so that you can stand to allow them—on the kitchen floor, on newspapers, in the kitchen sink. In good weather water play is a fine outlet.

It may not seem that you are encouraging a child's intellectual development when you permit him that much space, but in a real sense you are. What you are demonstrating to him is support for his earliest forays into the world. In a quiet way you give support to his trying things out and learning a few things for himself.

Safety, however, is not negotiable. We don't need him setting fires to learn that matches are dangerous. So it helps if the "no-nos" are clear. Covers over outlets help reduce the frequency of your prohibitions; medicines need to be under lock and key. Baby-proofing, or to be more accurate, toddler-proofing a house makes sense. It also frees you from supervising every minute and makes you less of a nag.

Distracting him with other things also can help in the

second year. It's not a method that works much beyond this time as he gets too smart for such handling. But at this age, when you often have to keep one step ahead of him to avoid disaster, it's not a bad strategem.

Keeping one step ahead of a toddler is a full-time job. There's no time for going to the bathroom, let alone reading the newspaper. In fact, going to the bathroom may be one of those freedoms you lose when you monitor a toddler. Once you close the bathroom door, it's as if bells ring, lights flash; . . . Mommy is needed at that very moment. You're less in control than you ever were because when they do something that requires your intervention, it means *immediate* intervention. When the lamp is about to topple over, you can't say to your child, "Wait a minute. I'm in the middle of an important call."

How about parental rights?

You *do* have some, although you might think from my recommendations that the toddler has them all. Not really. Each family will have to decide what its priorities are and what's off limits in *their* family. It may be the living room that's gated off or a fine couch that's a no-no. But the arguments will be fewer if you allow a lot more than you'd anticipated. A playroom in the basement doesn't usually work because the toddler loves to leave Mommy but he also wants to get to her as he needs to. So these rooms are generally unused unless Mother is down there, too. A room on the first floor can serve. Dining rooms become playrooms; kitchens, art studios. Apartments that have less space can still provide space for a child—a part of a room, toys behind a couch. If you can tolerate less attractive decor, an inexpensive couch can be a marvelous toy—especially during the long winter months when a toddler and mother can feel caged in. Jumping is a nice motor outlet when you can't get to a park. Also, cushions become playhouses; pillows, blocks.

Does this spoil him? I don't think so. Rather, it recognizes that he hasn't yet got the inner strength (he's too young) to resist so many temptations and he has to count on you to make clear what will wash and what won't. The freedom you allow generally makes him more agreeable rather than less.

Separation in the Second Year

Each new step in development brings progress but also confusion, because of the magical thinking of the under-two and three. Just when you thought separation issues were subsiding, he can again show worry when you leave. Now that he actually knows how to move about and move away from you, it dawns on him that you can do the same to him. Just when you thought you had it made, he can show old abandonment worries and shrieks when you go. The thinking of this age is described as magical because it rests on an imagination that has little objective fact to back it up. Here demonstration is the ticket and you can set up a more advanced game of peek-a-boo to help him work his way through the issue. In this game, you leave him with a known person, go around the block, and come back. He's beyond the thinking of the first year when he thought you no longer existed when he didn't see you. Now he just needs assurance that mobility won't mean losing you. You play the game again and extend the time each time you play it.

You say, "Mommy go away. Mommy come back." You leave your sweater with him or your keys. That's concrete. He's sure you'll come back for those. He has no sense of your having a life of your own (you may feel as if you don't) because he thinks egocentrically. "Nobody can see me," says the two-year-old who shuts his eyes.

When you carefully explain that you *need* to leave—that obligations call you such as work or school or even grocery shopping, he doesn't understand you. All he knows is how *he* feels. The exhilaration in all the new things he can do attests to his expanding sense of himself, but he suffers, too, because he is so vulnerable. His view of things is narrow and his perspective is limited. You see him at these times checking things out with you, touching base, refueling. You find you're as stuck as ever because he needs you at home base so he can leave you. A paradox. For the caretaker who substitutes for a mother at work, attention to the issues of separation is especially necessary. Chapter Sixteen addresses this in greater detail.

Negativism: Gaining a Sense of Self

A friend told me this recently about her son, age three-and-a-half. He had asked her where she was going after she left him at nursery school.

"I'm going to *my* school," she said carefully, "while you are at your school."

"No!" he said. "You go home. Make the beds." He wanted to be sure she was doing Mommy things while he was away.

This issue of self—who he is, how he is a special person different from anyone else—is taking place slowly in his mind as he absorbs and reacts to the many daily exchanges you have with him. As he wanders off he can differentiate himself from you. But since he isn't complete yet as a person, you see him coming back to make sure of things. He is attempting to straighten out his not-infrequent mental mix-ups.

For this reason he needs lots of things explained to him. The noise of a vacuum or a thunderstorm can frighten him. He can worry about going down the drain. In the latter case, the toddler's distorted sense of size is apparent. He not only gets time wrong—he also has size wrong. A mother may even see a temporary resistance to baths because of this. Explaining he is too big to be flushed down a tiny opening may or may not be understood. Sometimes only action helps (like a sponge bath on a lap) until his mind catches up with the facts: forward two steps, backward one.

This spiral view of development can help you at the times your patience is sorely tried by your toddler's inconsistency. He's not back to step one, as you may fear, but rather dipping back temporarily as he struggles with his unique and primitive ideas of how things work.

Learning to talk is an enormous help in this connection. You are guessing less about what he means as he puts words to meanings. (Books, stories, and games are learning tools but nothing beats conversation at this time of life.) With language, a mental thing (words) substitutes for a physical thing (action) and the beginning of abstract thought is a possibility. His growing vocabulary and the power it exerts in his little world is nothing short of spectacular. For now he has big magic. He wants cookie. He asks for cookie. He gets cookie.

Sometimes.

Frustration when he doesn't get his way is something you also see in the second year. The "terrible twos" are real and they can show up anywhere between eighteen months and three years.

The negativism that occurs in this period cuts across neat classification. As with all categories that describe human behavior, there's a lot of give at either end.

You will recognize the terrible twos *whenever* they appear, for he says "no" to everything. You have to remind yourself repeatedly that it's not just ornery negativism but this person's pride in his developing sense of himself.

"Do you want to go to the store?"

"No!"

"Don't you want to wear your nice new coat and hat?"

"No!"

If you take him firmly by the hand, he will put on his hat and coat and go with you. Here, again, actions speak louder than words. What he means by "no" is that now he is his own person. He can thwart the big giant who seems to be the boss of everything. The message about this time of life is not to take him too seriously. He wants to make things a contest but the less you get embroiled in his "I won'ts," the better for everybody. It becomes clear to you how conflicted a person the toddler is at this time of his life. He says, "I love you, Mommy," and then moments later he will try to sock you. Often he can't even agree with himself. Again—less intervention is better. When it comes to things that really count, you are bigger and you are the boss and it's okay to insist.

Preparation for toilet training can start at about eighteen months (even a bit earlier) if he is ready for it. That is to say, your child is able to say a few words that indicate he understands; he is walking; he is dry for several hours at a time. These indicate a readiness for the task at hand. It requires also that you be ready for it—you need to recognize that this is a process that usually takes time. Your availability and consistent expectation make it an important learning experience for your toddler. How you proceed can make a difference in his mastery of it. For this reason, I have devoted separate chapters to the question of toilet training because it is really the first time you are asking your child to do something *your* way. For the most part up to now you have been the giver, the helper, the good guy. Now the roles have shifted. You are asking something of him. This brings a shift in the power balance.

You can ask that he do what you request, but he has the final say of whether he will or not. Given the toddler's potential negativism, it is usually not an easy time for mothers. Hence the separate chapters that are specific about means of accomplishing training and explanation about the psychological benefits that accrue when it is accomplished.

The recommendations given work *with*, not against, the normal maturing of your child. You want him to be responsible for his own body functions, for his own sake, and you would like to be free of smelly diapers for your own. The two wishes are not incompatible. Actually, they work together. One of the first aims of toilet training is to help your child achieve independence. The more he does for himself, the less you are involved. So every measure recommended in those chapters leads to helping your child master the process for himself. What you will be doing, in effect, is providing the props so that he can take over. But since a child is growing all the time, a gradual increase in your expectation goes along with his ever-increasing abilities. At the same time that you help him be responsible for himself, he is growing older and more mature. This means that you take new measures as you progress. You require more of him as he matures. His attachment to you is an important element in his relinquishing his pleasure in messing and being contrary. One sees his wish to please as he struggles with all sides of his feelings.

"Yes?"

"No?"

"Maybe?"

Some have suggested that my recommendations about starting toilet training between one-and-a-half and two years of age come too early. Parents have reported that the process seems shorter if one starts later. They may be right. Everyone's child is different in this regard and you have to feel your way in this connection. But I have thought that trying to start the process before the terrible twos hit may make it a better learning experience for your child in the long run. If you can see it as a growth step for your child and not be too concerned about accidents (Chapters Three and Four are quite specific in how to handle these), the method I suggest may keep you out of what, in the long run, is something only he can do. How long it takes is less of an issue than what he is learning as he faces the issue of mastery of his body functions over time.

As your toddler moves beyond his second year, one

can literally see the emergence of a person with his own style, own way of adapting. Your being there to allow the quintessential person to evolve has given him a basic start. The year coming up will finalize a lot of what he's been given. And none of this, of course, has happened in a vacuum. It's been you and the toddler—he as explorer, you as protector and interpreter. If he wants to scale the mountain because it is there (as many older than he have sought to do), remember it is the provisions of the home base that enable him to attempt that summit.

3.
Toilet Training, Independence, and Responsibility

"W HEN I grow up," Laurie announced one day, "I want to be a baby."

Well, why not?

She, who had just mastered using the toilet properly, was now being urged to dress herself, brush her teeth, and stop whining. She had just had it with having so much to do.

A four-year-old I know put it differently.

"You know," he said to his mother, "how you said I would be much happier when I did what I'm supposed to do?"

"Yes?" responded his mother.

"Well," he snapped, "I'm not."

Parents, being the child's first educators, are not always popular when they support a more mature level of functioning. This is where the year from two to three (again with much give at either end in the sense that growth spurts vary from child to child) is different from the first two years. For this is the time that one's role as the child's most important educator comes to the fore.

The child who came to know and rely on you in the first year and then coalesced into more of a separate person from you in the second year, needs you to expect more of him, particularly in the area of body mastery and self-control in the third year. He is now integrated enough and loving enough for you to ask more of him and to institute some changes in his life. It helps him to know that even as he occasionally behaves intolerably, he feels safe in his world because he really knows you love him. And will forgive him. His tie to you hasn't faltered permanently despite temper tantrums (his and sometimes yours). There is a sense you both share that he *can* come into favor again. Your rift on a bad day is not irreparable. So you see him toward the end of the second year as having moved to a point where he can manage more, where his mental, physical, and emotional equipment has progressed significantly.

However, he can still be pretty irrational.

"*You* didn't cool the outside!" hissed three-year-old Jeremy at his mother when he ran out of an air-conditioned house on a hot August day.

Or Sally, who screamed at her mother when her ice cream cone fell.

"Me want it!" she yelled.

"You can have mine," Mother offered.

"No! Me want dat one!" as she pointed to her vanilla cone, now melting in the street.

It should comfort you to know that your relationship has a solid foundation despite times like this because progressive development occurs at both bad and good times. In toilet training, this relationship can often be sorely tested. You may ask your child to perform properly, but he not only has the final say about whether he will or not, he has the ultimate weapon. The balance of power in your family is now altered because you are put in the position of a requester, a "please do it in the pot" person. He who now has a vocabulary consisting largely of the word "no" can say so very emphatically. As we know, a child tends to be most negative (the normal phase at this age) just about the time you decide to toilet train. Sometimes he behaves as though being asked to give means being asked to give in. So the issue of conflict has to be faced. Do you push in the face of this resistance? Some child-care experts advise you to stop toilet training and wait until he is more ready. But when is that? These are a few of the issues that seem to make a normal step for your child a source of discomfort for you.

What Toilet Training Really Is

Toilet training is not just teaching your child to be clean. In a real sense it is not a training process at all. The phrase itself is incorrect for it reminds one of training a pet where you offer rewards for submission and punishment for mistakes. That concept, necessary for Fido perhaps, leaves out the idea of a self in the little person you are trying to train. It may work (and often doesn't) in getting a child clean but it leaves out what toilet training is really for. What it actually does is help character development. For toilet training is more than training; it is the first step in a learning experience that continues for the rest of your child's life. It is his first move toward becoming responsible for what he does, and it sets a precedent for future learning. It is, then, more of an educational process than anything else.

It helps if you can regard toilet training as part of a child's evolution. Through the process of training, you help him take steps to be clean for *himself.* What goes on during the process is as important as the results you hope to achieve.

For most children, this learning process takes time, often many months. It is not an isolated aspect of growth. Your child gains self-control in many ways (these are the side benefits) as you expect more and more of him over time.

Preparation for Toilet Training

You will be ready to start when your child shows some readiness for training. As mentioned earlier, he should have some words at his disposal. He needs to be walking. Some evidence of the ability to stay dry for a few hours gives you courage to begin since you know he has some control.

Also necessary for the undertaking is your own readiness to start. That is to say you need to be ready to undertake the steady expectation the process requires. If you are very busy with other things, it will be hard to give this the attention it needs. So other pressures of daily life need to be put on the back burner. Your being at home so you can keep an eye on what's happening is of first importance. Father and babysitter need to be tuned in to what you are doing so there is some consistency of management. But one person sets the agenda and runs the show so that everyone gets his signals clear.

You say there never is a right time? You have a point. There is always something—visitors coming, a new baby expected, or the house being painted. The trick is to find a relatively uncluttered time that you deliberately eke out of a busy schedule. Toilet training takes effort and it is hard to concentrate if there are many other things going on to which your child must adjust.

Toilet Training Equipment

The following purchases are designed to help your child achieve independence and mastery of his body functions. There are three steps to begin with:

1. Buy a potty chair. The pots with outhouse-type seats are useful because the child can reach the seat without your assistance. This saves a lot of unnecessary involve-

ment on your part and allows the child the feeling of mastery over his own territory. He is now at the stage of "me do it" and it is very nice to set things up so that he can. Small seat attachments to the big toilet may also be used, but since young children have difficulty reaching the toilet and sometimes fear falling in (the distorted sense of size from which they suffer still operates), a potty chair is often better. However, if your child prefers to use the regular toilet, don't make an issue of it. Just have a step stool for him to climb up on to reach the seat attachment you have provided. The idea is to have him manage it alone.

2. Buy many training pants (perhaps twelve to begin with) and buy the best pants available. These will be tight enough to hold accidents in and loose enough so he can pull them up and down himself. "Best" does not necessarily mean most expensive, merely put together well so that leakage is reduced. (This also reduces your anxiety about the messes you will encounter.) Boxer-type shorts and jeans with elastic tops are helpful for both sexes. These, too, can be easily pulled up and down. Zippers, suspenders, and buttons merely get in the way at this time. Here again, you've set it up so that he can handle it himself.

3. Buy a sponge. The old diaper pail can serve nicely as a bucket. You've been soaking his diapers in it for what feels like years. This will now be used for soaking the training pants, which are the diapers' successors. The sponge is for mopping up mistakes.

A Beginning Timetable for Toilet Training

Somewhere between sixteen and twenty-four months you start with some preparatory talk about body functions. The time you start has as much to do with you as him, since your attention has to be focused to enable him to understand what you expect. Name the functions for him. You can use family euphemisms like "dudu" or "tinkle" or "wee-wee" or "poop." Every family has its own terms, and far be it from me to insist on "BM" or "urinate." It doesn't matter what you call the functions, but it is important that you name them as he performs them.

This is an introductory time and you leave him in diapers as you put the new potty in a place where he can reach it easily. For those who use disposable diapers, the method is the same. At first, you suggest to him that he sit on the potty seat with his diapers on. That's to get him used to it. Try to catch him occasionally to help him get the point. A red face or grunt may alert you to imminent action. Lead him to the chair, suggesting mildly that this is a place to perform. As you unfasten safety pins or undo Velcro fasteners, you say something like, "This is where you are to make dudu." You can inspire him further by saying, "Big girls and boys make it in here. When you are bigger, you will make it here, too."

At the most do this twice a day, allowing nature to take its course the other times. You don't want to overdo by being too zealous. Tell him what he's to do there (and most likely has already done) and take care of changing his diapers as you have in the past. That is it at this beginning time. He can watch you empty the contents of his diapers into the potty so that he sees what goes where. Even disposable diapers can be emptied so he sees the connection. It's preliminary and it sets the stage for what comes later. What you are doing is letting him absorb a coming change in management in a fashion that allows him to catch on to the idea.

Six weeks or several months later the real effort begins. Before eighteen months his muscles in general are not mature enough to operate with control. So waiting until this time makes sense because now he can cooperate with you. Biology is in place. Kids vary, of course, in their readiness for this, just as they vary in beginning to talk or walk, but somewhere in the second half of the second year, they are usually ready. Children are different, too, in their tendency to be balky at this time. Many hate to be interrupted when they are doing something else, so try to choose the time for the trek to the potty with some tact. Don't be discouraged by lack of interest. It's a venture that requires patience. There is a human tendency not to like change, and your showing him something new brings normal resistance. That is why time spent in this preparatory way is useful.

Toilet Training Steps

You are now ready to make your expectations clear.

1. Place the potty chair in the bathroom. If there isn't a bathroom on the first floor, put the potty chair somewhere he can get to it easily. A hall or corner of the kitchen may not be too aesthetic, but they have their merits in that toddlers stray but always come back to where Mommy is.

2. One day you say: "You are getting to be a big boy now, and so Mommy bought you these new training pants." You show him the pile of pants in the bathroom or wherever the potty is located. He is sure to be intrigued. The quantity alone will dazzle him.

He may not say much but he's taking it all in because a great deal of understanding precedes speech. "And so," you continue, "I'm putting your diapers away because you can now wear big boy pants and do your poop and pee-pee in the potty chair all by yourself."

You demonstrate by putting the diapers away on a high shelf. Look confident and pleasantly authoritative but not too beseeching. Don't let him get the feeling you care too much. If he ever gets that idea, he can bedevil you when he is angry. Then point to the potty chair and say, "Do it here." And, "This is where big girls and boys do it." Show him how easy the new pants are to slip up and down.

Generally he will smile benignly, step delightedly into

31

the new pants, and promptly wet into his socks. Sneakers are a boon during this irritating phase.

3. Put away his plastic or rubber pants. This may sound destructive, particularly if you are devoted to your carpeting, but there's a sound reason for it. If his training pants are cozily tucked inside his rubber pants, as his diapers used to be, he doesn't know what's happening. He is not sure whether he has done something or not. Without the protection of these, his attention is drawn to the sagginess and/or smelliness of his training pants and he knows that something has happened. It is upon this gradual awareness that you begin to capitalize. You can still keep a few pairs to be used at nap and bedtime since training at those times comes later. Disposable diapers are less successful in teaching this lesson so you may want to use regular diapers for this phase.

In the baby days before training pants, he was quite content to stay in his messes and passively acquiesce to your changing him. The situation is now altered as he begins to feel the consequences of what he has done. The new discomfort, of which he gradually becomes aware, is a factor in his learning. Some children seem not to mind the mess and that can upset you. But if you stick with this method, you will find that eventually the mess is a constructive teacher. For the time being you are allowing him to suffer the outcome of wetting and soiling.

Unfortunately, you too will be experiencing the consequences. I admit it takes courage to let Junior soak into whatever he's standing on. You are a homemaker as well as a mother, and if you've worked hard to get that handsome carpet in your house, it may seem quite absurd to encourage your toddler to spoil it. But any permanent damage can be prevented. Baking soda or salt, when sprinkled over the offending spot, makes both stain and odor disappear. For new carpet owners who may be even more fastidious, a mixture of one quart of warm water to two tablespoons of white vinegar and two tablespoons of detergent makes an effective spot remover. Keep a bottle of the solution made up in the kitchen; this may help you deal more calmly with the results of a messy bottom and the owner of same. Club soda has proved useful in this connection too. It works well on both stain and odor. One mother recommends scotch and soda. The scotch is for you and the soda is for the spot.

The reason I am so explicit about how you handle the messiness is that it is essential to allow your child to take this step. By your not being overly concerned about accidents in the beginning, you start a process where he becomes the one to be concerned, not you. You are not vulnerable to the emotional threat of a dirty upset. You are able to keep your poise in the face of the possibility of messing.

4. It's a step in the right direction when he starts using the proper word for the appropriate function. Unfortunately, this may be *after* the fact. "Dudu!" he will shout ecstatically as he runs around the house alerting Daddy, and any other captive listener, to this marvelous accomplishment. Sometimes when he is more verbal he says, "Dudu, potty," indicating he knows where it is supposed to go. This doesn't mean he is doing it in the right place. Still, some connections are being made. He is making some inferences for himself.

After several weeks of this you begin to say to Junior, "Next time, tell me *before* you make dudu." When you hear a grunt or recognize a pre-pee-pee expression, say matter of factly, "I think you have to go to the potty now." Lead him to it and help him take his pants off, if he doesn't resist you—but then leave. Pray silently if you wish, but that is all.

5. Don't cajole him, or read him stories, or tell him he'll

get a treat if he performs. That removes his responsibility from the action. He then performs for the treat,
rather than because it's a job that must be done.

Do tell him he's doing it right when he does, but refrain from praising him extravagantly. After all, it's not
really an uncommon accomplishment.

You can say something like, "What a big boy you are!
How pleased you must be with yourself." This is a
sneaky point. It tells him he is to be congratulated for
what *he* has done. It praises him for *his* success in doing
a "big boy" thing. It isn't saying, "Please, pretty please,
do this for me."

Now, all of us mothers *feel* our children should perform for us. If our thoughts could be written over our
heads as in little comic-strip clouds, they would be saying, "Please, please, dear child, do it for me." And, "I am
sick to death of all this mopping up."

Or, "I am tired of chasing wiggly, stubborn, uncooper-
ative toddlers who keep saying 'no' to everything."

And, "Whatever happened to that darling baby who
was so sweet and adorable?"

Or, "Certainly he can't be teething at *this* age!"

But you persevere and several months after you've
begun with training pants you see that he seems to understand what you mean. Nevertheless, he doesn't seem
to be cooperating, despite your educational efforts. As he
soils your rug or wets the newly washed kitchen floor,
smiling beatifically at you and the mess he has created,
you may begin to feel a strange dislike for this once-loved
child. This is the time for positive action.

6. Give him the sponge. Tell him he must clean up his
mess. An important concept is demonstrated here. It is
the idea of consequence following act. You let a normal
function occur with the idea that he will slowly see the
connection between what he did and the undoing of
same. He is being allowed to be responsible for himself.

He is a toddler and no longer a baby. He is ready for more responsibility as each month passes.

The cleaning up may not be so clean; you may want to do it over yourself. You can, later. But at the time you say, "Billy made the mess. Billy clean it up!" You can add, if you're still coherent, "Next time Billy does it in the potty like a big boy."

In the cleanup demonstration you calmly show him how to:

a. Rinse his pants in the toilet. (A wire brush is useful here.)

b. Soak the pants in the diaper pail.

c. Pick up any assorted leavings with a tissue.

d. Wash the spot with a sponge.

After the first or second delighted sloshing in the john, he will find this pretty onerous. No child I ever knew enjoyed cleanups after the first few weeks. When he can't go outside without clean pants, he'll make some connections for himself. The idea of consequence following act is built right in.

Sometimes battle lines are drawn. You say, "Do it!" He says, "No!" You say, "Potty." He soils his pants. Try to avoid the battle by choosing your own good time for a confrontation. When the lady outside is honking her horn and Junior has to be ready, you can't very well make his cleaning up a major issue. He can refuse and you are pressed into doing it for him. Plan ahead for a confrontation in which you can't be blackmailed. For example, a trip to a friend's house can be canceled if your child isn't ready and hasn't cleaned himself up in time to go. Usually, one or two of these planned-ahead confrontations are enough to get the point across. You cannot force him to clean up, but you can build in some negative consequences for him if he refuses.

It takes time after you start him on cleanups; it may

take months. What makes it worthwhile is his slowly dawning awareness that he is responsible for what he has done.

As one little girl said, "It's my job." When a child masters toilet training and is finally clean, he is very proud. His self-esteem is very great, and it is his victory, not yours. How much sweeter for him! Often, after success is achieved, the "tricycle syndrome" may be observed. Body control in one area gives him the boost he needs to try in others. He mounts his bike and shouts with glee, "Look, Mommy! No hands!" His pride in his ability to control his body functions gives him the confidence to be more venturesome about other skills. The cleanliness achievement is only part of his success. The mastery of self is the greater gain.

7. After a time, allow him to take the step of emptying the contents of the potty into the toilet. He may prefer to delay this for a while and he may not want you to flush the contents away immediately. Again, the child's immature thinking that this "into the pot" business is a great accomplishment can influence you to delay flushing for a time. First he hears, "Oh, how grown up you are!" Then he sees "Whoosh!" That these productions of his need not really be saved takes a bit of comprehending. When he is used to going by himself, he can be asked to empty the pot himself.

Sometimes parents see a spurt of aggressive behavior at a time when their child has finally made it—that is, he has achieved success, is genuinely in charge, and very pleased with being clean. Why should this be, they ask. Here again is demonstrated the push and pull of normal development. The idea is not to pay much attention to the behavior because it won't last. Every time a child takes a really big step forward, there is often a flurry of infantile behavior that seems to need final discharge. Sometimes one sees this slip backward just before the final advance. One may also see regression when a child is under pressure in other ways (starting school, new siblings, etc.). These are all temporary slips. Often the last thing gained is the first thing lost. Try to be casual about these regressions. Children come around as the stressful time passes.

4.
Toilet Training: Overview and Later Developments

*O*NCE you begin toilet training, prepare to stay with it. It may take three to six months to achieve the desired results. Even with normal setbacks in daily life, the quiet carry-through you are involved in leaves an impressive message with your youngster. If there is an illness, unexpected guests, or other disruption in routine that upsets his progress, don't revert to diapers. Stay with the plan but allow for some adjustment. For example, if a child has a bout of diarrhea, put on two pairs of training pants, even plastic pants if needed. But don't reverse your stand on his giving up diapers. By not changing what you expect of him, you show your confidence in his ability to get back into the swing when the illness is over. Continue as before, recognizing that although he won't do as well for a while, this is only a temporary setback. Pick up where you left off and keep going. The worst that can happen is that the training may take a bit longer.

The idea that the child is a genuine participant in the training process is a new one to most parents. So be patient if others criticize your approach. When you see toilet training as an educational process that affects your child's total development, you will feel that the extra months and effort are worthwhile.

To Recapitulate

As you look at the process as a whole you can see that the actual training is being done in three steps. Children vary in readiness but this general guide for all children is helpful.

First, the preparatory stage: There is the telling him what he's supposed to do and the showing him where to do it. He's still in diapers then so you don't press him on all fronts at once. The functions have been named, and he is encouraged to sit on the potty chair. After a time, the diapers are removed as he sits. You still do the cleaning up.

The second step consists of the introduction of training pants. You make the trek to the potty twice a day. (I suggest limiting the amount of urging because getting after him all day long can provoke unnecessary resistance.) It helps if you keep an eye on him because you do better when you are aware of his need to go. The phrase, after a month of messing as you continue to clean him up, is "Next time tell me before." This is teaching him to connect the urge with the act and to take responsibility for it. At each step you include him.

Finally you expect him to clean up. You show him how to do this, having provided supplies ahead of time. In the beginning you give him assistance in wiping and clean-ups, but gradually you allow him to take over more. The temptation to go back to diapers after a stretch of not getting anywhere may be very great, but back and forth is a mixed signal to him. So once you begin, go for broke. Your determination in this is catching. He knows you are serious, and he feels more secure about his chances of succeeding. The use of plastic pants is a bit of a retreat, but whoever said consistency was completely possible in this less-than-all-perfect world?

If by chance you have let things slide and your child is three-and-a-half and you're still waiting for a sign from him that he's ready, don't wait. Start. You have to take the initiative. Don't be dissuaded by teasing, orneriness, and evasion—the usual lifestyle of toddlers.

Your toddler can say stubbornly, "I won't clean up," as one little boy I know did, adding to his mother's chagrin, "It's the Mommy's job." He can say it, of course, but don't you be the patsy and follow his advice. It's not good for him and it certainly isn't good for you.

How do you get a two-year-old to clean up? You are not really expecting a clean-up job; you are expecting participation in *his* cleaning up *his* mess. You *can* help him. It's not that hard once you get over thinking of your child as a baby. You will recognize that he can do it when you make your expectations clear. He understands more than he says, and he is taking a lot of his cues from you. He will respond to the consistent expectation of your tone.

Often mothers of boys delay training because they have been told boys are slower in this connection. I'm not sure if there is any real evidence to support this, but I do know that a mother's resolve is sapped if she doesn't believe in her child's capability. An expectant attitude is better for both sexes, and I would expect as much of a boy as I do of a girl. A confident attitude on your part helps a lot, for children pick up indecisiveness. What works is the fact that every time he makes a mistake, he has to face up to it. Learning proceeds, if in a zigzag fashion, when you allow this to happen.

Later Steps in Toilet Training

Bowel control may precede bladder control, although children vary in this regard. The point is not to count successes on a daily basis but rather to feel the child is moving in the right direction over a period of time. He is drier this week than last or this month than last, for example. Some children may attain bladder control at night as well as bowel control. But I would go slowly regarding nap time or night training. Keep plastic pants over training pants at nap time and bedtime and don't expect him to stay dry at those times. You can't ask him to do too many things at once.

Once he has mastered day training fairly completely, and you see occasional dryness at night, you can begin to let him take responsibility for night wetting. This generally happens between four and five years. Tell him this is the grown-up way. Remove the plastic pants and announce that he can get up to go to the bathroom. You can say, "You are managing the potty during the day like a grown-up boy. Now you can do this at nap time and bedtime." Let him know that he is allowed to get out of bed if he needs to. Ask him if he would like a night-light to help him to his destination. You can suggest a flash-light, which might be fun for him.

Another alternative is to put the potty in the bedroom —if you don't mind having it there at night. He can empty it in the morning.

Choose which aids work best for your child. Tell him about these proposals ahead of time so that he sees their connection with staying dry. In fact, every time you take a step with him, be sure to tell him what you're doing. Even if you're not sure he comprehends it, tell him anyhow.

Sometimes wetting or soiling at nap time and bedtime is a way of evading toilet training. If so, discuss it with him. "You're not supposed to do this in bed; you're supposed to do it in the potty." If he persists, stick to your expectations. Have him take off his own linen if his bed is wet or if he soils. You can help him with this. He can put his sheet in the bathroom or in a plastic bag you provide. No scolding or admonishing is appropriate. Gradually you step up his part of the clean-up. He can take the bag to the laundry room for eventual washing. The school-age child can be asked to soak his sheets, eventually putting them in the washer.

Here again it's his own doing.

This is only partially true, of course. You stack the cards by having him feel the discomfort of his mistakes. But at least he is presented squarely with some of the choices available to him. If he prefers messiness for a while, this is okay too. Young children normally go through a stage of enjoying messes. You can stand it if you know it's a temporary phase. The learning for him comes in having to do his own cleaning up.

Sometimes children play with their stools. This is a misconception of what stools are, and you have to correct it. If he starts to mess in this fashion tell him "no." Get him some clay. Tell him in true Haim Ginott fashion that "clay is for playing—BMs are for the toilet." Clean-ups should be encouraged by you but done by him. Don't be too concerned if he's not too neat in the beginning. He'll improve as he gets older. An assist from you is all right, but try to be less and less involved as time goes on.

Don't be concerned with how long it takes. The date of your child's success is far less important than the process by which he learns to achieve it. In fact, it is the process of coming to terms with cleanliness that makes this method so valuable. This should help you withstand criticism from mothers who claim more rapid success. Many children complete day training by age two or two-and-a-half; others take longer. Night training generally is not accomplished until four or five. In fact, occasional accidents continue to occur up to the age of six at various times of stress, even during the day.

Your son may prefer to stand up to urinate. Some mothers use a piece of toilet paper in the potty as a target to aid him in directing his stream. That's fine, but don't worry about it or press for it. Deflectors on the potty take care of this problem in the beginning if he is willing to sit down to urinate. However, if the deflector is so unwieldy or sharp that it is an obstacle, remove it and encourage him to direct his stream downward. "I hold it like a pencil," said two-and-a-half-year-old Mark. Later, when he shows interest he can be encouraged to perform standing up.

Emotions and Training

Psychologically, the toilet trainee is going through a period of conflicting desires. On the one hand, he loves you dearly and very much wants to please you. I don't want to dwell on this because an oversolicitous mother can come to feel that the child is demonstrating his love for her when he performs properly. You want to allow it to be his business, which in the most basic sense it is. Yet, in the background, his love for you does play a part. That is why your positive expectation counts more with him than anyone else's. You carry a weight you don't even know you have.

The other side of the coin is that he is now his own person. From a passive, compliant, and cuddly baby he has become a mass of resistance and "nos." Suddenly, when you try to diaper him, he arches his back with leonine menace, bouncing all over the bed to escape you.

The pattern of complying sometimes and refusing other times reflects an inner struggle that has nothing to do with you. He is learning some things for himself, and he has weighty questions to answer.

Yes?
No?
Will I?
Won't I?
Here?
There?
Now?
Later?

Don't be afraid of his anger, which will pop out from time to time. Anger is a normal emotion and a young child can feel it as much as anyone else. There will be moments when he gets pretty mad about having to clean up. It is human nature to prefer that someone else do the dirty work. Your firmness about this being his job, no matter how upset he is, helps support his growing character development. We all have to do things we don't want to do.

One two-year-old cleaned up her BM mess agreeably enough, but then crayoned the bathroom wall with her mother's best lipstick. Her mother went into the bedroom to cool down. (Fifteen minutes were required to prevent infanticide.) She then said to Ellen, "You made a mess because I had you clean up your BM mess. Now you must clean up this one too." (Lighter fluid is great on crayons and lipstick, though the child should use it under supervision, of course.) She and Ellen cleaned the wall together.

She then used a story to help Ellen understand her "I won't" feelings. (See Chapter Eight on the use of the Parallel Story.) She told her daughter that sometimes Ellen didn't want to clean up and sometimes she did. Sometimes Ellen wanted to be a big girl and play with toys and visit friends. But sometimes she wanted to be a baby and have Mommy clean up for her, like Mommy used to do when Ellen was a tiny baby.

The story acknowledged the child's conflicting desires —the wish to be more grown up and take a progressive step and the wish to have things the way they used to be. Her mother remained firm in her expectation and did not let up on the request. She did acknowledge Ellen's contrary feelings. Knowing that her mother understood helped Ellen to continue the training. Understanding does not mean yielding, however.

While anger is a normal human feeling, the two-year-old seems particularly prone to give vent to it. It's as if this particular emotion is somehow connected with his growing independence. Don't retreat in the face of it. It is not good for children to avoid responsibility by bullying. The fact was, it was Ellen's job. The feeling was, she didn't want to do it. The final outcome—she did it. The ultimate feeling—she liked herself better for doing well.

Those who promote a casual, laissez-faire approach to child rearing often forget the value of pride in achievement. Allowing children to *feel* negative emotions doesn't mean that we let them off the hook in terms of expectation. But living up to expectations takes time. Once you realize this, it's easier to be patient. The struggle the child is undergoing is important education for him.

A Word about Enemas

It is important to avoid enemas and suppositories. To a child, an enema is an overwhelming assault. Perhaps a story will illustrate what I mean.

A four-year-old girl was given an enema, and a severe withholding problem ensued. She withheld her BMs for two weeks at a time. It took many weeks of talk on the mother's part to undo the distress and anger of this child before she was able to resume natural functioning. Trying to feel less responsible, the mother told the child that Dr. Green had recommended the enema, which was indeed the case. A year later this little girl asked her mother in a conversational tone, "Oh, by the way, did they ever let Dr. Green out of jail?" That's what she thought enema givers deserved!

Make clear to your doctor that you are opposed to anal manipulation as a way of helping bowel function. Most doctors will agree to the use of oral stool softeners or extra fruit. After all, what goes in must come out. Recognizing that fact may make you less tense about your child's performance. Some children perform daily; others have only one or two BMS a week.

Another word about this sensitive area. Rectal thermometers can be frightening to children. Oral or underarm temperature taking does away with a lot of unnecessary anxiety. Many hospitals have already recognized this and no longer use rectal thermometers.

Again, I urge you to recognize that your child's progress will waver. Sometimes you have to beat a strategic retreat—for example, if he gets sick or you have to visit your fastidious Aunt Hannah so you put him back into plastic pants for an afternoon. Sometimes he won't clean up his mess and you end up doing it, though you know you shouldn't because you're being backed into a corner. But company is coming and there's no way out.

Expect that there will be days when he won't clean up, that there will be accidents after he's trained, and that there will be times when you can't see a single reason why he didn't do it in the right place. But don't pull back from your expectations. Despite setbacks, you will find that his own will is your best ally. And the great thing about this method is that it makes toilet training *his* responsibility, not yours.

In much of the literature about child rearing we seem to have lost the idea that the development of the will, of willpower, is an important part of growth. It is not that it isn't valued by all of us who work with children, but rather it is inferred rather than made explicit. Toilet training that encourages the child's will as he himself faces alternatives (and very real consequences) helps strengthen that will in a realistic way. So while he ultimately yields to societal pressure for cleanliness, he is not submitting because he has been threatened or bribed but because he is helped to confront the reality of the reality. He cooperates because he sees the connection between what he does and what follows. This is an early precursor for what happens in school later. Excuses are out as the child learns slowly that it is up to him to meet requirements. Gradualism aids the process and keeps him from feeling stressed. He learns he can do it. And the process is all.

5.
Discipline: Necessity, Dilemma, and Myths

*W*HAT is there about seeing an infant that makes us all melt? I have never seen it fail. A mother pushing a baby carriage is besieged with "What a darling!" "What a cute little pumpkin!" Grownups of all shapes and sizes become fairly daffy in the face of little fingers, sober stares, and toothless grins. In addition to the gratuitous advice a new mother receives—"Isn't she too cold?" "Isn't he too hot?" "Don't the twins need sweaters?"—there is the cooing, gurgling, baby talk of all the adults surrounding baby, determined to win a special smile from him. It is a nice phenomenon and reflects, I think, a tenderness toward the young of the species that serves them well in terms of firming our commitment to them.

It doesn't stop there.

Visions of sugar plums dance in our heads as we parents project their futures. Loving times around the family dinner table (glowing maple and candlelight), shared experiences and fun, appreciation and caring. We are star struck. Each couple is convinced that their special love for their special child will make for happy child rearing, free of conflict and the difficulties they hear about in other homes. This sentiment is shared by most of us in the beginning. That it is a Utopian fantasy (Utopia once being defined by a wit as victory without battle) we cannot foresee. For what it does not prepare us for is human nature, a state of being that includes the awfuls as well as the wonderfuls. The awfuls are anger and aggression, and it is they that cause the difficulty. Love is the mortar binding us together, but it is insufficient in itself to ensure the good behavior of our young. Adherence to a standard is a hard-won accomplishment and has to be taught. This is why discipline (Latin root meaning teaching) is necessary. And has always been so.

In 1871 a mother was reported asking her minister for help with an unruly child because he didn't "render a ready and willing compliance."

"She forgets," writes Jacob Abbott,* "that the faculties of reason and reflection and the power of appreciating the necessity and propriety of things, and of being considerate of future, remote and perhaps contingent good and evil to restrain and subdue the impetuousness of appetites and passions eager for present pleasure, are *qualities that appear late,* and are very slowly developed in the infantile mind; that no real reliance can be placed upon them in the early years of life." He goes on to urge parental guidance during this time of immaturity.

I couldn't have said it better myself (though perhaps more briefly).

Or as Bill Cosby is said to have remarked, "Give me two hundred two-year-olds, and I can conquer the world."

So our task as parents is to teach our children to be better than they are. Conflict is real and the only Utopians you will ultimately know are the folks with many

---

Gentle Measures in the Management and Training of the Young (New York: Harpers, 1871), 30. Italics mine.

opinions but without the chastening experience of being parents themselves. Everyone else is having the same troubles you are, in truth—kindness and love, disagreeableness and temper tantrums.

If you invited guests for a weekend and they never appeared on time for meals, unceremoniously turned their cups of coffee over on your best white tablecloth, grabbed for your phone before you could get to it, and never cleaned up after the messy bathrooms they left behind, how soon would you invite them again? How devoted would you remain?

Chances are your friends do not behave this way. Adults are relatively socialized. That's why they're easier to have as friends. But our children are not our friends—they may be someday, but not now. We didn't select them, and we didn't choose their qualities or even how they looked. We got them, even prayed for them, or perhaps discovered too late we were having them. Fortunately for the human race, there is something maternal or paternal in most of us, and we are able to be loving at least part of the time.

The Myth of Unlimited Love

Yet the myth that parents should always feel loving and never feel angry at their children is a fairly pervasive one in our society. It is responsible for a great deal of parental confusion and anxiety. The discrepancy between this perfectionist dream of how parents are supposed to feel and what they truly do feel makes for a lot of misery.

This would not be so hard to take if children would respond to the reasonableness we ask of ourselves with a corresponding reasonableness of their own. But they don't. And the fact that we don't respond reasonably when they don't (almost a certainty) derives from the fact that it took us a long time to grow up. There is nothing that can make us regress into infantile behavior more quickly than the infantile behavior of our very own young.

"I'll whomp you but good!" shouts a mother as her son tips over a stand of Campbell soups at the supermarket. With cans rolling in every direction, she is embarrassed, and she wants vengeance and she wants it fast.

Terry, age two, spread talcum powder all over the living room rug. "Look, Mommy, footprints," she said as she tracked the powder all over the house with her socks and shoes off, toes wiggling in every direction. Next, Terry smeared Vaseline all over the bedroom furniture. "And," she exclaimed with a pleased smile, "I polish." In the face of company coming to dinner in fifteen minutes, her mother could take no more. "I screamed like a banshee while my poor child cowered in a corner," she told me. "What made it worse was the fact that first I was mad at her. Then I was mad at myself. After all, was it her fault? She was only a tiny tot and trying to help." The mother described her unhappy ruminating. "I thought to myself, how could she know it was wrong? And even if she did, maybe she was angry because I'd been gone all morning." By the time Terry's mother got finished with her inner soliloquy, she had yelled murderously, vacuumed compulsively, apologized profusely, and then found herself in the uncomfortable state of not knowing what the issues were or how to deal with them effectively. An exhausting business.

The Myth of Childhood Innocence

Terry's mother was struggling with two not uncommon mixups that frequently cut into reasonable discipline. The first one concerns the child's innocence. Did Terry know or not know that what she had done was forbidden? At the age of two, perhaps not. But it still was reasonable to remove her, clean the place up, and fume. After all, company was coming and time was short. The mother went further, however, and made the inference that if Terry didn't know, she was then not responsible for what she had done. From there the mother took the step of blaming herself for being so angry, since she didn't approve of angry mothers. Mothers are supposed to feel loving, right? They are to be helpful and considerate at all times, correct? The issue of Terry's misbehavior was quite forgotten in all of this. The question of how to educate her to do better was lost in the guilt that confounded the mother because she was so angry.

The second mixup in this mother's reasoning concerned the child's motives. The mother speculated that Terry might well have been attempting to express a feeling by her behavior. She then made a psychological deduction that took Terry off the hook a second time. "If she's upset because I left her," thought this modern mother, "then I must be understanding of her motives. Poor darling, it's not her fault."

Either way Terry's mother approached the problem, her reasoning led to guilty feelings and self-recrimination. She was caught between "She's innocent so it's not her fault" and "She has a reason so I must forgive her." Her scolding of Terry had a no-yes, no-yes quality. Uncertainty had done her in—and there's nothing like uncertainty to do anyone in. Children are quick to perceive it, and then they move in with steamroller confidence.

What Terry's mother didn't know was that two-year-olds have limited ability to understand. Whatever the reason for the messing (adorable as it was deemed later in cocktail party conversation), Terry had made a mess, and her mother needed to stop her and, in doing so, teach her some restraint. With more time at her disposal, she could have had Terry help her clean up. She could have said, "Sand is for playing; powder is for baths." The emphasis would then have been on the act; the responsibility would have been on the child. The mother's job would be to instruct her, so that she would know better next time.

The Myth of Childhood Innocence with which this mother struggled supports the notion that little ones grow beautifully and naturally if the environment allows them to develop without interference. As with flowers, tender loving care is thought to be enough. There is little, if any, recognition of socially unacceptable impulses on the part of the young. The entire emphasis is on the role the environment must play to allow growth to emerge unimpeded. But what this idea does in actual practice is to paralyze parents. They wait to take their cues from their children, who are really waiting to take their cues from their parents. Everyone is in a fog.

The Understanding Fallacy

The second error in reasoning with which this mother struggled might be labeled the Understanding Fallacy. This view, unlike the first, acknowledges that children may be naughty or unreasonable but then *understands why and explains it away.* Once again, response to Junior's behavior gets lost in excuses ready-made for him.

Three-year-old Lee dumps his chocolate pudding on his baby sister's head. "It was an accident," coos Grandma sympathetically. "Here." She seizes a cloth. "I'll clean it up."

Mother, who has read many of the experts' books, bides her time. Later she gently explains to her mother that Lee is jealous of the new baby. Her mother, eager to be noninterfering and hence as popular as possible, looks blank. She struggles with a concept hitherto alien to her own child rearing. Are the little dears really capable of the hostility her daughter is suggesting? It is hard for grandmothers to remember back. If it's true, as Lee's mother says, that behavior has meaning and that a lot of what children do is not haphazard accident—what are parents to do in the face of such behavior? Do children have a right to be aggressive? This is one of the paradoxes in our age of psychological enlightenment. What was meant to be helpful in child rearing (the concept that children are really people, with complex feelings of their own) now is a dilemma for the adults who must rear them.

If Mother subscribes either to Grandmother's "He doesn't know any better" theory or her own "If he has a reason, he shouldn't be curbed" school of thought, her goose is cooked. If the child becomes aware that the adults in his world don't mean their "don'ts," he can push even harder to find out where the limits really are. Instead of better-behaved children, one gets children who are less well behaved.

The truth is that young children *can* be charming and lovable. I myself find them so, especially during naps. But it is also true that they can be mercilessly demanding and annoying no matter how sweet, understanding, and reasonable you are. A good deal of development has to take place before they learn to be considerate of their fellows. And the adults who raise them must do a good deal of teaching if children are to develop the self-discipline that will enable them to cope when parents are no longer there to oversee.

This is a different view from the one that sees discipline as unnecessary because "man is good" and will be self-disciplined as a matter of course. It is also different from the view that advocates a generally inflexible type of discipline because "man is bad" and needs to have the badness drilled out of him.

Children Are Neither Good nor Bad

Both of these extremes ignore the basic fact that a young child is incomplete. He has the potential for both goodness and badness, but he does not yet have the mental or emotional equipment to make sound choices. He needs older people with more experience to help him along.

When he makes mistakes or misbehaves, we have to remember in this age of popular psychology that a reason
is not an excuse. A reason may explain why something
has happened, but the doer is still responsible for what
he does.

Many parents believe that if they set a good example
by their own civilized behavior, their children will follow suit. Certainly this is part of the process, but it is by
no means all of it. What parents learn, often the hard
way, is that good behavior has to be taught.

To begin with, the very young child, adorable as he
may be, is a fairly unreasonable creature. He appears to
be quite certain that the world revolves around his
needs. A cry brings a genie bearing food, a whimper
brings a change of clothes, a shy smile yields hugs and
kisses from giants who kneel before those tiny fingers.

For the preservation of the race, it is good that babies
evoke this caretaking from all of us—or they would
never survive. The interaction of love and affection between the generations (no gap here) helps children to
develop the humanity and the caring they will pass on
to *their* children, for love runs downhill.

But love, as a famous doctor once said, is not
enough.* Good conduct has to be taught. In our twen-
tieth-century zeal to individualize children and respond
to their needs, we have often overlooked their equally
important needs for expectation, limits, and discipline.
As a result, many polite, loving, and charming parents
are so fearful of being considered "rejecting" (the final,
most horrible reproach in our current lexicon of name
calling) that they accept anything and everything their
children do.

"What can I do with him?" asks a mother helplessly as
she sees her five-year-old chase her three-year-old with a

*Bruno Bettelheim has written a book with this title, *Love Is Not
Enough* (Glencoe, Ill.: Free Press, 1950).

hot poker in his hand. "Grab the poker!" I shout, as I seize the three-year-old. "Stop him!"

I see her slowly absorb the idea that small children need limits. (The children are still alive at this writing.) Someone with more sense than a young child has to say "no." The child's very helplessness requires that the adults in charge serve as his steering mechanism for quite a while. The slow and gradual relinquishing of this steering function, as he gets older and is more capable of self-management, is what discipline is all about.

Motherhood Isn't Sainthood

The myth that mothers will always be kind, maternal, and patient during this process crumbles before the reality of human fallibility. Motherhood doesn't bequeath sainthood. Those who aspire to the latter may have a rude awakening.

Janie, five, was sent up to bed twenty times in a row. First she was down for a glass of water. Second for her teddy bear. Then the bathroom, next a kiss to Grandma. Then the bathroom again. A second kiss to Grandma. Her mother remained sweetly reasonable throughout this performance. At the nineteenth request she blew her cool. "How many times have I told you it's time for bed?" Her gentle tones had become a roar. She was shaking now with not-so-suppressed rage.

Five minutes later the final blow came. A curly head peeped over the bannister. "If you'd only said 'no' in the first place," said Janie piously, "this wouldn't have happened."

It was this mother's belief in the Myth of Childhood Innocence that put her in this fix. She was patiently waiting for the much-touted goodness to emerge and was setting a good example by her patient and reasonable tone. Janie, on the other hand, wanted what she wanted and even what she didn't want—a characteristic of the five-year-old and under. She needed someone with better sense to set her straight and mean it.

Small children can be untiring in their pushing. As one mother told me, "Give 'em an inch and they'll take a yard. And probably your neighbor's yard as well!" But if you think ahead to where you are going to set the limits, you can outline your strategy and step in early.

By making up your mind and stating that once out of bed for water and the bathroom is enough you are drawing the line for your child. Janie responded finally to the finality in her mother's voice. This could have happened, as she explained, nineteen times earlier. You do better when you make your expectations clear in the beginning, before you become so angry that nothing short of drawing blood will satisfy you.

The Unconditional Love Trap

One of the nicest mothers I ever knew was struggling with what she was learning about human nature in the cauldron of daily life with her three children under five. Usually the scenes occurred on the turnpike when she was returning home from an outing with them and could do nothing about the mayhem in the back seat. On one particular day, she had to swerve twice to avoid accidents when the oldest began punching his three-year-old sister. Her nerves were raw when they reached the house and she found herself practically throwing the five-year-old into the doorway by the scruff of his neck.

Several minutes later he came up to her sobbing, little chin quivering.

"You don't love me," he cried.

Mother folded him in her arms and assured him she loved him very much; she just didn't like what he did.

When she told me the story, I just looked at her.

"Well, what should I have said?"

"You should have said," I told her, "*you* weren't being lovable."

In our zeal to offer our children emotional security, we often lose track of who did what to whom. Making up with a hug is fine—no use prolonging the mads if we are really over them. But parents need to know that their educational efforts will be heard better if we stay within the facts. Her son had drawn her away from the issue of what *he* had done. After all, he had provoked her by *his* unacceptable behavior. The important gain for a child is in his regaining favor by improving *himself*, not sidetracking the issue by questioning Mother's loyalty. Conditional love as well as unconditional love helps the growing-up process. For the caretaker attempting to help a child be responsible for his actions, the job may be harder. She may not carry the same authority for the child. Here the support of her efforts by the parents is essential.

Responsibility Must Be Taught

Your child feels safer with structure in his life. I have seen many out-of-control children in my practice, and I find that they are really begging to be stopped. You do better when you stop them sooner rather than later.

The bonuses of this approach are the following:

You are less angry.

He is more lovable.

If the mother in the previous section had recognized how mad she was getting and stopped the behavior in the back seat (perhaps by pulling over to the side of the road), she might have been less physical with her son and therefore less guilty. She might have been better able to resist his victimizing her with his accusations because she had stopped the escalation before her anger took over. Accountability, not blame, was the issue here. Knowing where one's flash point is and getting below it can be useful. This means recognizing one's own escalating feelings and stepping in earlier.

Parents have argued with me about this point. They've said, "We've tried it. It doesn't work." When I ask them what happened to make their attempts fail, I learn that they tried the rule once, or even twice, but never for the weeks and months that it requires. Their uncertainty about whether they had a right to make their expectations stick showed up in a kind of pleading. Children, as I've said before, catch on pretty quickly. While the parents are waiting for sweet reason to emerge, the children see no cause to give up immediate pleasure unless it is clear to them that they must.

It takes time to teach responsibility, and your efforts are often not appreciated. Your child needs to know that his parents are in reasonable control of his life for a good many years. Children have few inner controls in the beginning. They learn about them, at first, from you. They are relieved when you take on this responsibility. And, over a period of time, they begin to take your rules and regulations into themselves. A slowly developing conscience (coming from the inside) gets its boost from you (acting on the outside) at a time when conscience is a variable and sometime thing.

The Myth of Natural Goodness (logical sequel to Childhood Innocence) contributes to the confusion of parents, for it robs them of decisiveness in the face of infantile behavior. It also conflicts with our well-documented observations of the egocentric infant. One little boy, age five, told me this quite clearly. He had been brought to see me because of his out-of-control behavior in kindergarten. "I want it all," he said, his arms circling an imaginary globe. "I want to be *first;* I want to be *best;* I want to be the *most loved;* I want to be the *most important.*" His behavior testified to this. He tormented his teacher and his classmates. He couldn't wait, or take a turn, or share a toy.

How do we reason with such a child? How do we help him accept the frustrations that go with recognizing the rights of others? How do we help him face the tensions that come when egocentricity demands modification? In short, how do we help him move from the pleasure principle of babyhood to the reality principle of life?

The next two chapters take up the question of the theory and practice of discipline. They could be titled, "How to Civilize Your Child Without Taking the Joy out of Him or out of You Either."

6.
Fundamentals of Discipline

"*E*VERYTHING I do," says Tommy indignantly, "you blame on me." Hands on his hips, eyes close to tears, he is very, very sorry for himself. Yet he cannot join in our laughter. He doesn't see the point.

Two-year-old Mary, having just wet herself, points to her friend Betty accusingly. "Her did it," she says. "Her wet my pants."

The question of who did what is a big one, and the matter of responsibility in some instances may never be resolved satisfactorily. But all parents are confronted by the question of responsibility, and discipline is the means by which they help instill a sense of responsibility in their children.

Discipline, in its most elemental sense, means teaching. The ultimate aim of discipline is to make the child responsible for himself and his behavior. The long-range goal is the child's self-control. The problem then becomes one of how to shift the controls from yourself to him. What makes the situation complicated is that the child is growing and changing all the time. Trying to keep up with him is like trying to catch a moving train.

You have to change your expectations as he develops. The signals aren't always clear.

"It's Just a Stage"

Pediatricians sometimes assuage parents' anxieties about their children's development with the comment, "Don't worry. It's just a stage." They have a point. It is not only the child's bones that are growing but his mind and awareness too. Growth, both physical and emotional, *is* a factor and it is on your side. It proceeds, normally, in the direction of maturity. Many of the quirks of the two-year-old do pass. That the three-year-old only develops new idiosyncrasies can be frustrating. One of the most difficult things for a mother is getting used to this constant change. Just about the time you think you've figured out how to deal with him, he's off on a new kick. It can be pretty exasperating. As the main educator of your child, you are placed in the position of having to teach what you believe is proper behavior. You don't always know how to go about it. Some kids pick up what you expect with little direction. They are the ones who irritate every other mother on the block. Most kids aren't that easy to teach. For your peace of mind, don't compare yourself to the mothers of these paragons. Cultivate the mother who's in worse shape than you are; she could really be a friend.

Helping a child become self-disciplined requires effort. The experts who discuss motherhood as a self-fulfilling experience don't seem to recognize the hard work involved. Teaching is required, and the best kind of teaching occurs when the child sees a connection between what happened and the results that follow. A sequential kind of reasoning begins to take place.

When a child is very young you have to intervene frequently, and the reasons for your actions may not be clear to him. But you can't allow him to discover the danger of cars so he will learn to stay on the sidewalk.

As he starts to get about on his own, at the end of the first year or the beginning of the second, it's a good idea to toddler-proof the house. This is a sensible recognition of his immaturity. Removing dangerous things ahead of time saves a lot of wear and tear on both of you. As he grows older and gains more impulse control, he will be able to manage better. His safety—which includes putting poisons out of his reach, holding on tightly to his hand as you approach a street crossing, strapping him in when you drive in a car, and the many other things you do to protect him—requires commonsense stratagems that you employ without much thought. They attest to your acknowledging his immaturity. His life and safety require active intervention.

But after you've allowed for the stringent action you take on these issues, you are still confronted by the day-in day-out disciplining that your child requires. The need for your intervention comes from the normal antisocial feelings that accompany his growth and development.

Teaching Self-Control

There are some general concepts of teaching self-control that apply to all ages. Intervention means teaching right from wrong. If your child hits someone or tries to destroy something, he should be stopped. Remove him immediately, if not from the scene, then from the spot. If he goes back for more, take him home. If he's already at home, put him in another room. If he breaks something, explain that he has to make the loss good. Restitution can be made. He can go with you to buy a new vase or he can work with you to glue something together. There is a logic in making something good, in fixing up, in undoing a mess. If he embarrasses you while you are out, take him firmly by the hand—or sidesaddle if he puts up a real kick—and leave. No need to put up with supermarket antics. Cereal for dinner one night is better than a huge scene at the store. He learns a lot from these sensible consequences that you provide for him. He may not be able to see the larger ones yet, but as you step in as necessity dictates, he does begin to learn. He can be made to sit on a stool until he can manage. He can be sent to his room if he needs time to cool down. He can be told he can join you when he can control himself. The aim is always to put the responsibility on him—where it belongs.

This approach is positive because:

1. It makes the child aware that he is expected to do better.

2. It implies that he has the capacity to improve.

3. It enables him to see the connection between what he did and why he is being stopped.

4. It gives him a chance to think things over without a fight. He can't listen until he's calmed down. Often, when a child is put in a room, he begins to play and defuses by himself.

5. It allows him to rejoin the family when he thinks he can handle things. This gives him some feeling of power over his own destiny. He isn't merely giving in to you; he is meeting a social demand when he is able. The urge for self-control is given a boost since he likes himself better when he manages well.

This approach is also positive because it does *not:*

1. Hurt his feelings—at least not for very long.

2. Encourage the nursing of grievances and the desire for revenge.

3. Clear the air so swiftly he can promptly forget about it. (In one instance, Stephen, eight, was sent to me because he seemed to ask for spankings. He agreed that this was so. "It's simple," he said. "When I get one, it wipes the slate clean. It's my ticket to start over." He felt that he had paid—not learned, but paid.)

4. Set up a contest in which he ends up feeling like a loser.

The real battle for self-control is within the child himself. Partly he wants to grow up and do more; partly he likes what is easy, infantile, and familiar. If you allow this issue to get lost in a fight between the two of you, you end up taking the responsibility for what is his responsibility after all. Remember that the important argument is not between you and your child. It is between the child's two conflicting feelings. The ping-pong match should be with himself.

This idea may be new to you because often the idea of winning enters into a conflict without our being aware of it. Our own childhoods often reflect this. Some adult won and we as children submitted (since we had little choice in this regard). This does not mean we learned much from the experience. The better way, if you can see the point, is to stop the fight, remove the child, and allow him to rejoin you again when *he* improves. The issue of his regaining favor by modifying *his* behavior makes a real contribution to character development. And if he won't go to his room, you might go to yours. Some parents have argued with me about this, feeling that this means the child has won. I don't think so. The idea is to break the logjam and diminish the power fight.

Punishment

A time-honored method of discipline is punishment. That is, you instill fear into a child in the belief that this will deter him from future nefarious activity. It may. Parents have told me that spankings clear the air. I believe they often do. But I don't think it is the inflicting of pain that does the trick. Rather, what happens is that the child finally perceives that the parents truly mean what they say. Most often, spankings come as a last resort. We are at our wits' end. Nothing has worked, and we are really beyond reason ourselves. By this time we may want to inflict a little pain, especially because we are feeling so much of it ourselves.

Here teaching has been lost as everyone is out of control. A fight has ensued, with you the winner because you are bigger. One father told me with pride that he had thrashed his eight-year-old, who had hit a three-year-old, within an inch of his life. "I'll teach him," he said, "to pick on someone smaller."

Right.

If you plan ahead for the worst contingencies, you are taken less by surprise and are therefore less likely to spank. You are also less likely to threaten punishment that you won't deliver. If you do have to come down hard in the face of provocation, your response won't be out of proportion to the situation.

Making a Plan

Making a plan may mean sitting down with your husband in a quiet spot and thinking over what is appropriate for your child at his age. Going out to eat to talk things over often helps both of you to be more objective. When you are both clear about what you expect of your child, you can then make it clear to him. If you tell him ahead of time and give him sufficient warning ("We have to leave in half an hour so start getting ready"), he has time to switch gears and prepare himself.

The rules of the game are expectation, consistency, and stopping him when he can't manage. If you keep changing the rules on him, he'll be confused. You may be skeptical about whether this system works because you've seen your child repeatedly delay the family by refusing to be ready on time. Or you've seen him make a mess at someone's home and refuse to clean it up.

But you do have a surprising ally in all of this—your child himself. He has a wish to be good, to grow up and master things. Stopping him from behavior that is not socially acceptable enables his better self to win. It encourages the child's self-esteem, because there is pride in virtue. A child likes himself better when he knows he's done the right thing. A good thing to say to him is, "I won't let you do that because it will make you feel bad about yourself." This acknowledges conscience (developing slowly but nonetheless coming at this age) and supports impulse control. On the other hand, all human beings, big or little, get angry sometimes. Once we accept this fact we can begin to deal with the less than beautiful feelings more realistically.

Every parent has his own style. Some parents grew up with spankings and are not comfortable with other methods. Others try the "Get in early before you are unhinged" approach and find that it works. All parents, however, will help their children grow in the right direction by setting a goal ahead of time—say, for the next three months—and then requiring that it be met. The first step is to select the issues that are important to you. These vary from family to family. But you have the right to insist on what matters most to you. Once you have done so, you will find yourself able to be flexible about matters that don't mean so much to you. This flexibility helps the long-term firmness that is required.

Special problem areas run the gamut of childish orneriness. Holding the line on the issue that bothers your family the most is the best place to begin. It could be the bedtime issue that you choose to take up; it could be mealtime shenanigans; it could be changing clothes after school or, with older children, doing homework before watching television in the evening. It could be any problem that upsets your particular family.

When you choose the one that bugs you *the most,* stay with your expectations on that point over a period of time. And remember that you can't deal effectively with more than one big problem at a time. If you go at a number of them, the child feels he's being nagged and soon learns to tune you out. Staying consistently with the one problem, for months if necessary, will simplify life for the whole family in the long run. More important, the success achieved in one area will begin to spread to other issues. The carry-over occurs because the child has mastered something in himself in the process of dealing successfully with one issue. It's as though he's developing moral muscle when he succeeds in behaving better. Try to remember that the young child will do what is right as long as someone he cares about insists on it. Later, when he begins to adopt many of your values as his own, you will be able to lessen your active involvement.

Backsliding will occur occasionally, since home is not the army. But if the trend is in the right direction, you'll make your point. A good general rule, when you're choosing the issues that are helpful for his development, is never to do for a child what he's able to do for himself. A lot of nonsense gets eliminated by observing this rule. A lot of infantile tyranny dissipates.

Saying vs. Doing

Whatever your home environment, it does not hurt your child to be asked to fit in. You can hear little ones out; you can listen to complaints; you can even ask them for their ideas about what they can do to fulfill your demands. *But* it is your judgment that prevails when you think something is *right*. They do not yet have the overall picture, and it is important for you not to yield on something that you feel is not desirable for them.

"My Mommy means it," said four-year-old Lucy proudly to a friend. What she meant was that she appreciates her mother's caring enough about her to risk facing Lucy's displeasure. Wanting to be loved by a child can make you afraid to be firm. Don't let it! Children feel safer with clear-cut limits. While our ideal is to be rational and to give our children sensible reasons for what we expect of them, this can often be overdone. A clear "Because I said so" is often as reasonable as you can get, given the demands of family life.

This latter point raises an issue that bedevils all parents. One mother said to me, "If I let her say it, does it mean I let her do it?" The answer is no, you don't. The little girl can voice her jealousy of her baby brother. "I wish you'd take him back where you got him," she says angrily. She can announce that he is a pest and that she'd like to push him out a window. "But I won't let you," you tell her. "You can feel it and say it, but you can't do it."

This is the ultimate restraint. The talking provides a channel for the unacceptable feeling, but the controls are still coming from you. Some parents are reluctant to encourage children to voice their feelings in the fear that it will open a Pandora's box of bad behavior. On the contrary. The hurt and/or angry feelings are there anyhow. The acceptable outlet of talk can prevent mayhem, as it offers a release of pressure. By saying "We don't hit" and "I won't let you hurt me" and "Go to your room until you can manage," you put the lid on the behavior. At the same time, by showing the child that you understand, you make his difficult feelings easier to bear. Stories that illuminate a point for children are a great help in this connection (see Chapter Eight).

Special Issues at Two and Three Years of Age

Until the age of three most toddlers are not truly ready for interactional play with others. It is not that they don't enjoy being with other children. They do, at least for short periods of time. But most children under three indulge in parallel play. They look like they're playing with others but they're really playing side by side. The possessive, antisocial behavior the toddler shows about his possessions (toys, mother, *anything*) is par for the course until three or more. Don't wear yourself out trying to teach your child sharing before he is old enough to be able to cope with the garden-variety "I'm for me first" feelings. Of course, it doesn't hurt him if you work toward sharing and taking turns, but recognize that your successes will be tiny until he's closer to three.

On the other hand, hitting, biting, kicking, and grabbing are out. Don't hesitate to pick him up and put him somewhere else. Once again, stopping and removal work best. Talking about it after he calms down helps link the idea with the action. He is more able to tolerate a direct confrontation as he approaches three. He also shows some signs of having heard your prohibitions.

Andy, three, was heard to say to himself as his hand stretched toward a forbidden candy bar, "No, no! Andy mustn't." His mother's prohibition could be heard in his voice. Whether he could summon the strength to *really* resist was less the issue than that he had heard her and was trying to meet her standards. Most children of this age waver a great deal. Sometimes immediate pleasure wins; sometimes they can hold off. One way to help manage this with the two-to-three-year-old toddler is to voice the conflict for him. "Sometimes Andy wants to do what Mommy says; sometimes Andy wants to do what *he* wants."

Occasionally his provocation is hard to handle. His eyes dance delightedly as he tests you. He is trying to make a contest out of your prohibition. You might try saying firmly, "I don't want you to do that." Then leave the room. This allows the struggle to be his. Often he complies because you have taken the challenge out of it. You can always remove him if this doesn't work.

Refusing to be provoked by orneriness is easier said than done. Sometimes when you see yourself caught in a daily tangle with an autocratic toddler, you can consider whether it might not be better to sidestep some unprofitable struggles. Helping him save face may ease the hard-line stance you both find yourselves in.

"You can be the boss of wearing your hat," you say, or "of eating your carrot" or "of carrying your bear or elephant." He is old enough now to enjoy a decision that's his alone. "But we do have to go," you add, "so you decide about it now."

"I don't want my hat," says Jennifer as she takes it off and marches defiantly out the door. Some of the win-lose sting has been defused.

Be aware that a two-year-old's ability to stay with things is limited. Keep your visiting activities brief, unless your hosts are equipped and willing. Fatigue works against good behavior, so try to give your child his rest. Naps help him to tolerate the daily fray. When he starts to resist napping, set up a daily silent time. He can be permitted books and quiet toys in bed. If he flatly refuses bed, you might permit him to play quietly on the couch or floor. It is important that you separate from each other. You need the space yourself. If he complains about rest time, set a timer and insist on relative quiet until the bell rings. You might have toys available that are only used during these periods. He won't be happy if you are enjoying yourself too much, however, so keep your own enjoyment of these times a secret.

Three to Four Years of Age

Three to four is a great age for day-care or nursery school, if you can arrange it. A neutral teacher, with less of an emotional investment in the child, helps in the teaching of appropriate behavior. Cooperative nurseries, where mothers take turns, serve the same function. If neither of these is open to you, try to arrange for your child to play regularly with a small group of children. Learning to play with others is an ongoing process, and he is more ready for the give and take of social life than he was before. At this age, too, he can pick up his toys and do other simple chores such as emptying a waste basket and putting out napkins. A place to play with a chance to let off steam is good for both of you. Physical activity in a playground or yard is pleasurable for him and helps the discipline process.

Up until this point, you have talked with him primarily about real things in his life. He relates to objects and to people in a fairly concrete way. You may have talked about feelings to him, but you have been uncertain about how much has penetrated. Now he can begin to tell you his feelings as you encourage verbalization. You say, until you are sick of the sound of your own voice, "Tell me, tell me in words." If he is angry, reply to his complaints realistically. If his demand is unrealistic, don't alter your position. You may be able to help him accept your firm stand by telling him, "I know it's hard for you." Your understanding can ease the angry, hurt, or frightened feelings.

You are not encouraging feelings as good in and of themselves. They exist in your child as in all human beings; the idea is to make them manageable. As they are verbalized, he can get a handle on them. Hearing himself speak allows him to cope better and manage more successfully. It aids the civilizing process.

When Jimmy was two-and-a-half, he would shout, as he thrashed about, "I'm bangy." At three, Jimmy would glare at his mother menacingly, as he grew angrier and angrier, and yell, "I'm getting bangy." He was recognizing a familiar feeling and giving fair warning. His growing knowledge of his feelings allowed him to put on his coat as she'd requested. Before he had the words to make his point, he often banged his fists and head against the wall. The improvement in his ability to recognize where his feelings were headed was noticeable in this six-month period of development.

The issues of expectation and the setting of limits as they have been described here may seem reasonable to you. The rub comes in the contradictory nature of your child's progress.

"My son tells me he can't change his clothes. He acts helpless, wanting me to do it for him. When I don't, he cries and acts forlorn." This mother had thought that being firm would make her little boy feel unloved, since her expectations seemed to make him so miserable. When she learned not to play his game, she was amazed at how pleased he was with his own success. "Why then did he fight me so during the process?" she asked. Part of the answer lies in the fact that children prefer what they've known. The new step is threatening until it is mastered.

Again, it helps to voice a conflict for a child when he is going through a struggle. Tell him, "Part of you wants to be a baby; part of you wants to be grown up." Instead of fighting with you, he learns the battle is within him. The yes-no struggle reflects the inner battle that young children have in growing up. While you support the more mature requirements of good behavior, you help him verbalize his baby longings. A good principle to remember is that he does better when you align yourself with the part of him that wants to grow up. Throwing your weight in this direction is always to the good. Insisting that he do what you know he can do is realistic, and he respects you and himself more as you maintain your expectations. Your voicing the less mature wishes gives acknowledgment to his infantile side, thereby diminishing their intensity.

Four to Five Years of Age

Between four and five the child's world expands enormously. Friendships develop; play is more genuinely interactional and more reasonable. You try to help him meet the new and varied expectations that are being made of him. You end by being his backup as he tackles the new and, therefore, the hard. You teach him to cross a street. You show him how to tie his shoes. He can take a bath by himself (bubble bath soaks off what he misses).

When he wants to try something more adult, you let him do it, if it's within reason and if you see the justification for it. In these and many other ways you are supporting the development of a self that slowly but surely is becoming independent of you. Safety is, of course, a major factor, and you have a right to be protective.

"You cannot swing from the high swing."

"No, you may not walk on the railroad ties."

He still counts on your judgment, so feel free to wield it, even though he may balk and answer back.

Encouraging this new independence can sometimes be difficult. Four-year-old Nancy was upset about going to nursery school after an easy initiation. Her mother was bewildered. "Do I make her go?" she asked me.

"Is it a good school?"

"Excellent."

"Do you like the staff?"

"Very much," she said.

"Do you think going to this school is a good experience for Nancy?"

"No doubt about it."

I suggested that she tell Nancy she would like to hear more about why she didn't want to go. Perhaps she could confer with the teacher. But at the same time Nancy was to be told, "You have to go to nursery school. Daddy and I think it's good for you." This was not rampant authoritarianism; it was a wiser judgment than Nancy was able at her age to muster. Allowing her to express her feelings helped Nancy to cope without encouraging regression.

Holding the line is not easy for parents. In the middle of such everyday happenings as broken washing machines, delayed plumbers, mother-in-law visits, and laid-off husbands, clear reasoning about normal child development may be hard to come by. Having more than one child brings several sets of tracks—all, it seems, going off in different directions. There are times when you will be boxed into doing some things for your child that he can do for himself, in the interest of expediency and mental health (yours). There are times when yielding is an absolute necessity. Forgive yourself at such moments and get him back into training when things settle down. At frazzling times, an afternoon away in adult company can do a lot to restore your equilibrium. Visiting friends who have young children is also helpful, not only for the company but for the commiseration: you realize, with some satisfaction, that the same hassles are going on elsewhere.

7.

Discipline: Specific Behavior Problems and Means of Coping

*D*ESPITE the best of intentions, there are some things you cannot make your child do.

You cannot make your child eat.

You cannot make him sleep.

You cannot make him perform body functions.

When he is of school age you cannot make him study.

In every one of these cases it's the old story: "You can lead a horse to water, but you can't make him drink."

Parents, in a genuine concern over nutrition, have sometimes forced their children to eat; and their children have promptly vomited the food right back up. Wooing sleep, as most adults know all too well, is something that must be done by the sleeper himself. While toilet training is a normal process that I heartily espouse, in the last analysis the child himself must actually perform in the right place. The same is true of learning in school in the later years. You can buy a lovely home, provide a great room for your child to work in, select a handsome desk and the best sightsaving lamp, and he can sit amid this splendor and read a comic book or daydream.

Knowing your limitations in regard to these issues can spare you a lot of grief. It is a waste of effort and a sore test of your patience to take responsibility for those matters in which your child is the final arbiter. What can be done, as in toilet training, is setting the scene so that he, who has the final say anyhow, will handle the issue in a way that is constructive for him.

Eating

Physicians who have studied nutrition have learned that children will eat what their bodies require, providing (and this is a big if) that they do not fill themselves up with junk between meals. You can eliminate a lot of the nagging that goes on at many tables in America by serving food and then pretty much ignoring what the kids do with it. No, you don't have to put up with their slinging the peas or daubing their siblings with mashed potatoes. Removal is the best technique for dealing with that kind of nonsense. What I am talking about here is your concern over what they ingest. It's not that important.

This is a provocative remark to make in the face of this country's recent interest in nutrition. By saying it is not important I do not mean that you ignore what you know is best for him in the preparation of food. We have all learned about the four essential food groups and there is no doubt that we are eating more nutritionally today than we have in the past. But once we have shopped sensibly for the kind of food we think best (thinking of possible alternatives as we go), it is a good idea to leave the ingestion of that food up to your child. To do otherwise is to invite a fight you cannot win.

Milk drinkers, imbibing as they are the near-perfect food, often eat next to nothing. Food eaters often boycott milk. In addition, there are plateau periods of growth where children simply do not eat very much at all. Then at other times they gorge. Nature really takes care of the growth process, and it's a mistake to get too involved in it. If you begin to care too much, as with the toilet-training process, the child will learn how much he can control you with his response to your offerings. Let your doctor tell you if your child is deficient in anything.

Limit snacks to regular times of day—say, midmorning or afternoon—and keep a moderate supply of crackers or cookies around to serve with milk or juice. Don't keep fillers like potato chips, pretzels, and candy around. They simply tempt palates that are then too sated to appreciate your hamburgers. Eliminate the bickering by eliminating the temptation. If you or your husband want some special snacks, tuck some away.

When you serve a meal, give your child advance notice. "In fifteen minutes I'll call you in for lunch." When he comes in, serve it. If he complains that he doesn't like this or that, say, "Okay, then don't eat it." If he wants only dessert, let him have it. If you're very concerned about his nutrition, stick to fruits, puddings, ice cream, or gelatin for dessert. This doesn't mean he is winning a battle and that you are contributing to the weakening of his manly fiber. It does mean that you are not making a moral issue out of a natural process. Why should ice cream be less valued than broccoli? It, too, is highly nutritious. It is we who make these value judgments by announcing, "You don't get your dessert unless you eat your vegetables." When the fight goes out of it, children generally eat all food better.

Do *not* become a short-order cook. If he doesn't want to eat at mealtime, place his plate in the refrigerator. If he's hungry later, he can have it then. If he complains that the meal is cold, do not heat it up. If he wants a hot meal, he will have to learn to eat it when it's served. Here, too, the consequences are built in. If he misses a meal, ignore it. He'll just eat more heartily the next time.

As he gets older and displays a few marked food aversions, such as hating liver or getting a rash from fish, you can allow him to make a sandwich for himself when you serve these foods. The point is not to disturb the rest of the family but to recognize an individual bias when it is legitimate. Removing food as an arena for argument makes children less scrappy in general, so that on the issues where you really have to hold the line, they are more amenable to reason—as you are.

If you feel that you cannot offer dessert without your child's earning it (the Puritan ethic seems caught up in this for a lot of people), what you can do is serve family style. Family-style meals help to create a pleasant atmosphere, since children select what and how much of something they want. Allow the child to take his own helping from the family serving dish—as little or as much as he wishes. It is then his obligation to finish what he has chosen if he is to receive dessert. This is a second-best plan (the best is not caring at all), but it may be as much as you can undertake, considering the way your parents dealt with you.

Sleeping

Bedtime requires a similar approach. Deciding ahead of time on an hour that is suitable for your family is a good beginning. Sticking to it may be hard, as children "spoil" easily in this area. Staying up with your child at night during an illness may have him insisting afterward that you prolong your stay in his room. Get him back at once on an "out for a drink and bathroom" regimen, and that is it. Be oblivious to crocodile tears. If he complains he can't sleep, put a lamp near his bed and let him have some quiet playthings, such as cuddle toys, books, crayons, and paper. This lets him wind down, and you may often find him fast asleep over his toys in a few minutes. Nap time can produce similar resistance as a child gets older. Insist on a quiet time, allow for some play in bed, and place a timer in his room to let him know when he can leave.

Serenity has been defined as having an alternative. If he can't sleep, give him an alternative by permitting quiet play. Here again you set the rules and arrange the props; he performs the act. Once he starts school, he may try to beat the system by staying up to read. But here you win for losing because he is becoming a reader. In general, quiet times before bed are best; roughhousing should be kept to a minimum. There is nothing wrong with a toss in the air if the child enjoys it. Fathers often think this is a good way to relate to children and carry it further with tussling and wrestling. They think roughhousing makes men out of boys. But often children find it too stimulating, and sleep disturbances result. If you see this happening, try more quiet play before bedtime. Fathers can make contact with their children without overstimulating them. They can read them stories and help them with puzzles, and play other games with them when they are older.

Sports during the day are another matter, but children are better off engaging in sports activities with those of their own age. This puts them in a less disadvantaged position. For the child under five, games of chance are better than games requiring skill. In skill games competition with an adult is unfair, and it doesn't make sense for an adult to pretend to lose. In games of chance (like the various spin-the-wheel games) everyone is equal before the odds. The child may lose, but he may just as easily win. Hold off on skill games until the child is of school age, when he is more capable of grasping the concepts involved.

The importance of play in general is not negligable. The kind of "make-up-our-own-ideas" play that often gets lost in this busy world is valuable for children. Providing them with unstructured time offers them a chance to think their own thoughts, invent their own games. Play is not the opposite of a serious pursuit. It allows children a trying out of things, a taking of different roles. It may repeat painful experiences—undoing them and providing happier endings than reality affords. Mastery can be seen as they work things over piecemeal in their play. In a sense, play is a form of self-teaching, a making up for hurts and frustrations. One can often see the liquidation of anxiety as children work through a painful experience. Grownups' respect for free time gives the inner world of the child a chance to be thought through independently and therefore enlarged. The emphasis today on more and more activities for children, as if their minds were blank unless written on from the outside, is one of those swings (such as superbaby) that sometimes happen in American society. When we understand the needs of the whole child again this should right itself.

The issue of watching TV before bedtime is not a simple one. Each family has its own constellation of interests and must decide about TV for itself. Yet there is no question that TV sets up an artificial situation in which children are bombarded with stimulating material but are placed in the position of receiving it passively. For this reason children often indulge in thumbsucking, masturbating, eating, and nervous mannerisms while watching TV. The tensions, which have been artificially engendered by the media, have no place else to go. Cutting down on afterdinner viewing usually makes sleep easier. When you have a big family, this may be difficult to do. You are faced with individual preferences and who watches what, when. One mother of five got so fed up with TV bickering that she outlawed TV on school nights. She okayed it on Fridays and Saturdays, and the group voted on which shows were to be seen. She could not believe how much wrangling she eliminated in this way. What surprised her most was how relieved the children seemed to be and how easily they accepted her decision. Apparently a lot of covert sibling rivalry (endless in any family anyhow) found its way to the surface in the fight over choosing programs. With children under five it is easier to be selective because the good children's programs are fairly obvious.

Studying

The same principles that are applicable to body self-control apply to the issue of learning when the child enters school. Once again, your primary task is to provide an environment that will allow the child to take over the function for himself. Just as only the eater can eat, sleeper can sleep, and toilet trainee can train himself, so only the student can learn.

A boy in third grade came home one day with a note from his teacher. She was irate about his poor performance on an arithmetic test. When his mother criticized him, he argued his case plaintively, "But you never took the arithmetic problems out of my pocket!" He needed to be told that school was his business and that homework was his responsibility. In our zeal to help children learn, we have often confused the issue of responsibility. Our wish to rescue children from failure stems from the best of kindly impulses. Certainly there is nothing wrong with being available to help a child if he asks for it. But learning is clearly something he has to do for himself, and it doesn't help him when we accept it as our job. When he isn't doing well, confrontation by the teacher can be constructive for him. After all, it is she who is in a position to assess his problems realistically. As parents we can be sympathetic to his feeling of failure, but we help him best when we ask him what *he* is going to do about it. Even well-meant tutoring will not help if the child has no intention of cooperating.

Throughout a child's life the issues of reality and responsibility have to be balanced against immediate pleasure and gratification. Here again, consequences teach best. An early failure in school, if it is warranted, and repeating a grade can often have sanguine results. Admittedly, you will find it difficult to let this happen to your child because you care about him so much and you hate to see him hurt. It will help you when hard decisions have to be made to know that self-esteem comes from within. When a child masters something hard for himself, his pleasure in himself is genuine.

Performing in school is an area in which every parent has an investment. Sometimes this makes parents do more urging and monitoring of school work than proves productive. Children often are only too content to shift responsibility from what is theirs, after all, to us. (Shades of toilet training!) If you as parents can support the school in its efforts to insist on meeting expectations, the ball goes back to your child's corner. Any help you give him occurs because he requests it of you, rather than because you have assumed responsibility for what only he as a student can do.

However, there is a form of behavior over which you have to exert control—namely, antisocial behavior. You have control over whether your child is *permitted* to carry out his antisocial impulses. You are not only bigger, you have more awareness of what is right and what is wrong. Ultimately, you hope your child will take your views to heart and make them his own. But during the early years it is you who must step in and actively teach. Aggression in children takes many forms, not all of which have been recognized by parents. Fighting, of course, is the most clearly recognizable and may require your intervention if other children are being abused.

Fighting

The hitter or biter or scratcher is demonstrating behavior that is *actively* antisocial. Stopping the child and/or removing him from the spot works best. Getting him to talk about his anger when he cools down is helpful, for moving from action to words is a more mature development.

"Danny is mad," you say, as you label his feelings for him. "No, you cannot hit a person," you add. "People hurt when you hit them. Tell me when you're angry." If the child is very young, you can provide an inanimate substitute for him to hit, making the point that things, unlike people, don't *feel*.

If you find him tormenting an animal, stop that, too. "I think I'm raising a sadist," complained one father to me about his three-year-old daughter. She had been dragging the cat around, kicking it, and pulling its tail unmercifully. She was having a difficult time restraining herself in the tumult of a large family.

After some consideration, her father arranged to have the cat stay with a friend. "When you can manage not to hurt it, you can have your pet back," he told her. After several trial visits at home, the cat was allowed reentry. Margie managed better with each successive visit, and her pleasure in her growing self-control was evident.

When your child is older, the sequence will progress from actions to words to thoughts. He will then have the capacity for trial action by means of thought. He can *think* he'd like to slug his friend who received a bigger present, but he won't *do* it. Thinking can both *allow* the antisocial idea and *prohibit* the acting out of the idea. The child will then be able to behave in a more mature way under stress. In kindergarten, children are described as immature when they erupt into action every time they are frustrated. The delay that talk or thought brings is not available to them, and their learning is impaired as long as action takes over immediately. If the child has had practice in expressing himself, he has greater ability to delay inappropriate responses. Helping your child to tolerate some frustration aids his developing maturity. You can voice his upset.

"You wish you knew how to ride a bike. When you are older you will be able to do it."

"No, you must wait your turn."

"It's hard not to get what you want this minute."

The kindergarten teacher will be grateful if your child has learned to tie his shoes before he starts school, but she will be even more grateful if he has learned to tolerate some delay, listen to some instructions, and postpone a demand if necessary.

Hitting back if one is attacked is another question. Most parents see this as a reasonable response that builds self-respect and allows for sensible self-protection. What gets sticky is when the child says he was attacked first but he wasn't; then you are pressed to make a judgment about something you know little about. When you can't find the real culprit in a free-for-all, send everyone to different parts of the house to calm down. There are many battles that end up ambiguously, and a "so what" attitude on your part will probably save your sanity. "I don't care who did what," you find yourself saying. "Just cut it out!"

If you should happen to punish indiscriminately without knowing the facts, the child who is innocent will feel he has been treated unjustly, and your reputation for fairness will suffer. Stopping the children, scattering them, and allowing their anger to subside clears the air better. These storms are generally of short duration, and often the children are pals again before you've had time to regain your equilibrium.

Dawdling

The dawdler is of another breed entirely. He doesn't appear to be aggressive at all. He just takes twenty minutes to get a sock on, keeps you waiting while he searches vaguely for his gloves, or pulls a sweater on in cinematic slow motion while you steam. "He's a dreamer," you tell your friends. The inference is that he's thinking long, important thoughts. But he can certainly move fast enough when he wants to. What is going on here? He makes you furious, but you can't put your finger on it.

After all, he hasn't actually *done* anything—or has he?

My answer is that he has. He hasn't actively driven you out of your mind; he has done it passively. So innocently, so slowly, so seemingly not doing much of anything; and yet you are wild. My advice is to trust your gut reaction. Looking at his behavior objectively, you will see that he had plenty of time in which to be ready. He isn't ready. He provoked your anger by his delaying tactics; he has goaded you. That is really as open a challenge as outright defiance.

Eight-year-old Linda and her family lived right around the corner from her school, yet her mother had to wake her at six every morning to be ready for class at eight-forty. It took her half an hour to brush her teeth. Putting on underwear was a laborious task. At every step her mother reminded, prodded, and exhorted. The battle had to be rewon daily.

Things changed when Linda was told it was her business to get to school. Going to school was the law. She was given an alarm clock, which was realistically set for seven-forty-five; her mother retreated to a back bedroom. The first day Linda, at eight-twenty-five, was sitting in her pajamas waving to her friends who were on their way to school. Mother almost had apoplexy but instead had a third cup of coffee.

As her mother and I talked, she realized how her daughter had blackmailed her.

"But what if she doesn't have time to eat?" she asked, alarmed.

"Is she thin?"

"Oh, no. If anything, she's on the chubby side."

"Good. She can lose weight at the same time."

"But suppose she's late for school?"

"What then?"

"Why, she'll get a tardy slip!" Mother looked horrified.

Linda never did get a tardy slip. One day the policeman at the corner stopped her mother. "Say, listen," he said. "Is Linda your kid?"

She acknowledged that she was.

He scratched his head in a puzzled way. "What is it with her anyway?" he asked. "Every morning she walks like molasses to the corner. And then," he added with a bewildered look, "she turns the corner and beats it like a bat out of hell right to school!"

There are times, of course, when ignoring the dawdler will be impossible. You must be somewhere with your youngster at a certain time and he is stalling the whole family. A good technique, if you can set it up in advance, is to pay a sitter to stand by at her telephone. This makes sense, particularly for the under-five child, who does not have the same social obligations as the older child. Then if he is not ready on time, leave him home! You will rarely have to repeat this rather stringent lesson.

A timer may be helpful for the dawdler. Tell him you're setting it and he must be ready when it rings. If he's not, he doesn't go. The timer has the great advantage of eliminating your voice.

When faced with dawdling, I am often reminded of Eleanor Roosevelt's response to a niece who was bewailing the fact that she hadn't had enough time to do something. "But you had all the time there was," Mrs. Roosevelt said gently.

Selfishness

Three-year-old Don and three-and-a-half-year-old Carey were sitting side by side on the sofa, each with his arms crossed over his chest. Chins thrust forward, they both looked like thunderclouds.

"What is it?" asked one of the mothers.

"We both are *not* sharing," said Don.

Children over three can be taught to share, when mothers work at it. But even then, as every mother knows, there are days and there are days. Before three, sharing is very tenuous. The invited child, whose toys are not in question, generally does better. The host, who may be quite amenable to sharing at other times, may embarrass his mother with "It's mine! Don't touch that!" It generally takes some effort to appease the two factions, and sometimes you have to cut a visit short. When sibling rivalry is intense, displaced feelings may be put on a visiting friend, intensifying the "Leave my territory alone" feelings. It is important to realize that selfish feelings are normal and that more kindly ones will show themselves in time. Children between three and four develop genuine relationships with others and, in doing so, learn by trial and error about the necessity to give and take. You can voice their not-so-nice feelings for them in private if you wish.

"Sometimes you like to share, but sometimes you don't. Sometimes you want *everything* for yourself."

Talk doesn't change the necessity to share, but it does keep criticism at a minimum, thereby enabling the child's more generous emotions to surface.

Whining

One mother asked me to title this section "Cooking with Whine." She couldn't bear the querulous tones of her four-year-old as she tried to prepare the evening meal. Whining, like dawdling, is aggressive. It upsets you because it implies a hidden reproach. Since, like all mothers, you are extraordinarily responsive to even the most subtle of accusations (for the past thirty years mothers have been programmed to believe that almost everything is *their* fault), you berate yourself. Where have you failed? Why isn't your darling child satisfied?

Here the rights of mothers need to be invoked. Be blunt. "I don't like whining. Please tell me what bothers you or what it is you want." If the whining persists, send the child to his room and tell him to come back when he can talk normally. Like chalk squeaking on a blackboard, whining gets your back up. If it goes on, you get nasty —which only gives your child empirical proof of your unreasonableness. Tell him to cut it out before it gets to you. If he refuses to go to his room, pick him up bodily and put him there. If he won't stay, gate the room. Children feel safer when you mean what you say.

Verbal Abuse

Mothers who have encouraged their children to verbalize are often taken aback by a barrage of verbal abuse they had not anticipated.

"It's okay to tell me how you feel," says Jimmy's mother with a determinedly therapeutic gleam in her eye.

Jimmy brightens considerably. "You are a stupid dumbhead!" he shouts.

Mother, raised as she was in a more polite era, is caught off guard. She snaps, "How dare you talk to me like that!"

What happened?

Jimmy's mother mistook the use of words for genuine verbalizing. Sometimes it is the same, and sometimes it isn't. Words, when used to master a problem, as in the understanding of feelings, help the child to achieve self-control. But words can also be abusive and hurt another person. When this occurs, the child has to be shown what he is doing. "You are angry and I want to hear why," you can say, "but I don't like to be called names. It's not being nice to another person." The step from action abuse to verbal abuse, as in Jimmy's case, is a forward step in the civilizing process, but abuse is still abuse and a big mouth can be very hard to tolerate. It is a step toward genuine talking, but it is *not* what I mean by verbalization, and parents do not have to be subjected to it in the name of good child rearing.

If you don't like the insults and epithets you are being

subjected to, insist that these be hurled somewhere else. He can go to his room and shout imprecations. You can sit in another room and turn up the radio. It's no different from sending your child to his room when he can't manage his physical aggression. After the verbal tantrum is over, you can ask him what made him so mad. The beginning of genuine verbalizing is then a possibility. But real talk is never possible in the midst of battle, physical or otherwise. It is all right to treat verbal abuse as abuse.

Messiness

Leaving clothes on the floor provokes many fights between the generations. It is very difficult for a mother to see how she can let a consequence follow that teaches *him* when it is *her* house that is being turned into a junk pile.

For children over four the use of a box may be helpful. Get a large box from the supermarket and place it somewhere out of sight—the basement, a spare room. Tell the kids you are not hanging up their things anymore. When you find a jacket, a pair of shoes, underwear, or a scarf lying around, toss it in the box. *Eventually* they have to go to the box to redeem the article. Don't keep too many clothes around when you set this plan in motion, or your little girl may be wearing her best sleeveless dress to a Brownie cookout in November. Have a reasonable supply of a week's clothes on hand (put out-of-season clothes in an old trunk where your child can't find them). Then watch the process work. If he wants to wear a pair of summer shorts when the snow is four feet deep, tell him you're not about to let him get pneumonia. He has to wear regular clothes. When he protests that he has none, tell him they're in the box. When he argues that his wool pants are wrinkled, tell him to hang them up the next time. As with reducing fights about mealtime, he learns by experience. Eliminating your voice helps things along. He feels you are nagging when you keep telling him what to do. You can have a rule that your child can't wear dirty clothes to school. It is his job to put his clothes in the hamper. This rule is more successful with the school-age child than with the under-five child, who is not subject to the same social pressures as his older brother and sister. When your child is between two-and-a-half and four you will be washing his clothes almost every day, so the issue of neatness is largely your doing. However, by the time your child is three-and-a-half or four, you can insist on his bringing his soiled clothes to the hamper. He can be asked to put clean clothing away. He can also be asked to put toys away at night. Plastic containers, clearly marked, can help the sorting process. Much of what you require in these areas is a personal matter. But you have the right to insist on *your* requirements, since your child lives in *your* house.

A college girl I know recently couldn't find her good shoes. "Did you put them in the box?" she asked her mother good-naturedly. Shades of the past!

Temper Tantrums

Temper tantrums are storms that happen when verbalization has not taken place. Your child's feelings build, but he has found no way to discharge them. His pent-up feelings have nowhere to go, and he loses control of himself in flailing, fighting, and flinging himself around.

The first thing to do with the under-five child who is besieged in this fashion is to remove him to a quiet place. It will take time for him to deaccelerate, and you want to make sure he can't hurt himself. Stay with him if he's headed in that direction. Say "I won't let you hurt yourself," as you toss pillows under him. He feels safer when you take over the controls for a short time and let him know that he can call on some of your strength to weather the storm.

If the tantrum is of a milder sort, such as stamping his foot or shouting furiously, put him in isolation and then encourage him to talk. If he is still screaming, tell him you will talk it over when he calms down. You cannot respond peaceably in the midst of a hurricane.

Getting the child to acknowledge angry feelings, important in all discipline problems, is particularly helpful with the tantrum. The best way to prevent tantrums is to allow the child to express his rage in words at the time it is felt. When anger is emitted piecemeal through words, it need not erupt into something overwhelming that frightens him as much as it does you.

Remember, too, that during the course of their development children will have angry feelings that are quite unrelated to your handling—as in the case of the two-year-old's negativism or the four-year-old's attempts to play one parent against the other. These are normal phases that really do pass. Often the child himself doesn't know what is eating him. If he is unable to verbalize a feeling and you cannot locate a reasonable source, tell him that he is having a bad day or that he woke up on the wrong side of bed. After all, we have our bad times too. You can sympathize with him for the tough time he's having, but you can also make it plain that he's not to take it out on other people. A reasonable premise that covers almost every situation can be summarized as follows: You can't hurt me, yourself, or the house.

Remember that fatigue or hunger can exacerbate problems. Often a good rest and a full belly make a child more reasonable and available for talking. As with all of us, there are good and bad times for a discussion. Tact is appreciated as much by children as by adults.

Fears

Fears are not behavioral problems, but they frequently cause problems that require parents' attention. In infancy fears of falling and of loud noises are common. In the second and third years the bathroom is sometimes frightening. As mentioned earlier, children may fear being pulled down the drain or even being flushed away in the toilet. Since a two-year-old's perceptions of size differences are all askew, he doesn't know he is too big for the drain and may clutch frantically at his mother's knee in an attempt to avoid being put in the bathtub. The same youngster may fling himself unconcernedly into the swimming pool. Fears of vacuum cleaners, sirens, thunder, lightning, spiders, and bees are common and tend to come and go as young children perceive and misperceive the realities around them.

Parents who understand immature thinking take these fears seriously. Comfort and console your child, then explain the facts as they really are. "You can't go down the drain." If he clutches harder, you may have to add, "You're too big." If he is still unconvinced, tell him, "I won't let you."

Sponge bathing a child who suffers from such distorted views is not spoiling him. The fear will pass soon enough—and then you won't be able to get him out of the tub.

What if he fears imaginary intruders? Night-lights can help dispel them. Dogs, which children generally regard as four-legged people, are sometimes perceived as jungle predators. The child's emotional state can color the most benign objects with fright and horror. You hold to the realities. "The dog is just yawning. He doesn't want to bite." If he is frightened by a dog in the street, tell him, "The dog is on a chain. I won't let him bite you." Once again you are the voice of reality and the protector.

Fear of body damage comes up over and over again with each successive year of development. He needs reassurance. "No, your nose will not break off. The ashtray that broke is not like a part of you. People don't break."

Television programs can make for upsets. In some shows, arms disappear, people are decapitated, people are eaten, witches seem real. It helps to keep an eye on

93

what your children are watching because these programs, though presumably designed for children, often
contribute to unnecessary fears. Fairy tales too can be
very gory, but their effect on the child is moderated by
the teller.

With TV, you may be able to quiet fears by telling him,
"It's only pretend." If this doesn't allay his fear, teach
him to turn the set off by himself. "You don't need to see
that scary program. Let's turn it off." The active shutting away of TV monsters can relieve his sense of helplessness. The knowledge that fears are normal and that
they will pass should help you endure your child's inappropriate response.

Nightmares can disturb even young children. Their
immature emotional equipment creates distortions that
can wake them in a fright. Here, too, comfort is best.
"It's not real; it's a dream" can pin a name to an unnama-
ble dread. Sometimes you need to sit with them at night
until these dissipate. Greater maturity helps them cope
better, but nightmares will surface from time to time for
the rest of their lives.

Finally, let's not forget that children need privacy.
They don't have to tell us everything they do or feel.
They work out many of their problems by themselves in
the course of growing up. The recommendations I have
made in this chapter are designed to help provide a sensible framework for a child's life. They are intended not
to interfere with normal growth and development but
rather to be of background assistance.

8.
The Parallel Story: An Aid to Insight

Story time is enjoyed enormously by preschoolers because stories are *interesting*. They can tell about daily experiences in a child's life, and this affords the satisfaction of the familiar. Nursery rhymes and the simple classics you enjoyed as a child also give pleasure to *you* because they pass the culture down. Your child grows to love them just as you did. (Ever try to skip a page before the eagle eye of a three-year-old? There is no way to get away with this. He knows all the lines.) Imaginative tales are fun too—in these, colorful pictures and interesting events take your child along unfamiliar paths. He can soar beyond the narrow confines of reality. He can feel safe in your presence as the author describes things beyond his vision. For some parents this time is valuable, too, as an educational opportunity, for as you read to your child you are using words and showing him how important they are. He too will want to learn to read just as you did. There is big magic in books and a love of these can bring him pleasure for the rest of his life. And finally, of course, there is the giving of yourself, the giving of time.

Another use of the story is one I have found valuable in my work with children. This is the parallel story and is not meant to be a substitute for literature. This is a made-up story that addresses your child's emotions. As adults, we have learned that behavior means something. It reflects our inner lives, and as we develop as parents, we are more and more confronted by the behavior and hence, the inner lives of our young. On the one hand we have the not-so-easy task of insisting our children behave. It is this that allows our children to live in society and to function with respect for others who also have claims. Our role as educators is prominent here. As educators we may acknowledge the feelings behind the behavior of little ones but we find we must insist on some standards of conduct or our children do not develop the inner restraints that allow them to function successfully. (I don't know where the notion of mental health as a state of no-restraints got started. It certainly does not help a child become his more mature self.)

Yet the emotions of the preschooler are powerful, often like a whirlwind that lifts him beyond self-control. It is as if he hasn't the ability as yet (along with sufficient experience and intelligence) to control himself by himself. It is you who are a help to him in the early years, for you not only encourage better behavior by discipline appropriate to the age, you help him understand his feelings better by talking about them. This aids mastery.

The use of the parallel story is a stratagem then for reaching feelings he may not be able to express directly. In fact children are often loath to put feelings into words. They generally rely on behavior to express what they mean. The story is an interim means of telling a feeling *another* child has. For him the indirectness makes it more palatable. He can hear it better, for it's not getting too close to the bone.

Here are some examples of parallel stories.

"There once was a little boy. His name was Billy."
Eric, age three, gets closer to Mother on the couch.
"There was a mommy and a daddy living with him but
he was the *only child,*" she goes on. Eric nods content-
edly. This is the "Billy story" he has asked his mother to
tell him every night for the past two weeks. He knows
what she is going to say before she says it, but he wants
to hear what is coming anyhow.

"Billy's mommy used to take him to the store," says
Eric's mother. "They bought things to eat and Billy liked
to have his mother make him lunch." She enlarges on the
story and inserts elements of her own child's life into it.
"His favorite was peanut butter and jelly." She stresses
how much Billy liked being the *only one.* Eric is rapt with
attention.

"And then I went to the zoo with Daddy," he adds.
"Don't forget the monkeys." He likes the parallel she
draws because it gives him a chance to ruminate about
his life experiences. When we consider how much of
growing up is an assault on the egocentric position of
babyhood, we can understand his enjoyment of the story
better.

"And then came a baby brother," his mother goes on.
"Billy didn't like that one bit." Eric nods in response
to this. "The baby can't even throw a ball!"

His mother agrees. "Billy wanted a friend to play
with, and instead he got a baby!"

"Babies stink!" Eric's voice rises. "They make poop in
their pants!" His pride in his own rather recent accomplishment is evidenced in his disdain.

"The hardest part for Billy was that he wasn't the only
child any more. He liked being the only one. Before the
baby came he used to have his mommy all to himself."

"And you walk him while I'm at school!" The enor-
mity of her offense overwhelms Eric for a moment.

"Billy hated to be away. He thought his mother and the baby were having too much fun."

Why Stories Are Valuable

You get the idea. By telling a story you recognize with your child that emotions exist; you dignify them and admit your child's right to them. In this way you make his feelings more explicable to him.

In our parental role as educators we have little difficulty in telling a child about the real world. "This is your nose." "Here is your cup." We teach words for things. It is an objective process, and we move on easily to the properties of things.

"The stove is hot."

We take the next step and draw a conclusion for him. "You mustn't touch."

We stand between the property of hot and the consequence of injury. This is so self-evident it hardly bears examination.

But we often have great difficulty talking directly to the child about his emotional life. That is why the parallel story is so valuable. It is an educational tool that teaches him about his inner world. He learns about feelings. These feelings may have small relationship to the real world. Was Billy ever *really* the only one? Wasn't there a father and didn't his mother have interests of her own that had value for her despite his childish wishes to the contrary?

Tom Stoppard wrote a play* many years ago about the nonprincipal performers in *Hamlet.* Two courtiers, Rosencrantz and Guildenstern, heard only snatches of the main performers'conversations as they came in and out of the scenes. The real drama of what was going on in the play was lost to them since only part of the talk was heard. This is how life is for the child. His inability to

---

Rosencrantz and Guildenstern Are Dead (New York: Grove, 1967).

understand the total picture is a feature of childhood. In all of these chapters the message is the same. You are filling in the gaps he can't understand. With your better understanding of where he is in the process of development, you try to give him information that he can absorb. Knowing the normal distresses that most children are subject to in the course of growing up can give you clues. These provide the content of the stories you can make up to enlarge his ability to perceive.

Sibling Rivalry

Parallel stories can go in any direction. The young child's envy of an older sibling's skills can be dealt with in another story.

"Once there was a little boy named Johnny. He was three years old. He had a big sister, Ann, who was five. Ann went to school every day. Johnny liked to do everything Ann could do."

You take it from there and improvise with particular elements that are meaningful for him. "Ann could ride a bike and count numbers." You might pause here to see if he wants to tell you something. Sometimes he gets into the story, as Eric did. Sometimes he sits there blankly, and sometimes he runs around acting as if he isn't listening at all. Don't be discouraged. Often he never replies. This does not mean that he isn't listening. To your astonishment, he may ask for the story months later, or he may refer to it casually in another connection. But it is true that you may never get a concrete response. Nevertheless, go on.

"Johnny wished he could ride a bike. He wished he could do these grown-up things." It is not difficult to see that you are on target because Johnny has shown in so many ways that his jealousy makes life difficult for him. "It was hard for Johnny to wait until he was able to do the things that Ann could do." You may wish to rush to the happy ending. "But every day Johnny was growing

99

older. One day he was able to ride a bike. One day he could go to school and learn to read."

There is nothing wrong with a happy ending such as this. In fact, most children's stories conclude on such a note, with problems finally getting settled in a comforting way. But the strength of your made-to-fit stories is that you need not rush to make things okay so fast. Negative feelings, which most of us were not allowed to express in our own childhood, take time to unroll. In general, because of our own rearing, we don't like to hear about them either. Everyone wants things to be harmonious and serene—particularly grandparents and well-meaning friends who prefer the untroubled surface of things. What they don't understand is that negative feelings exist everywhere, whether the feelings are acknowledged or not. If you understand that your child's acceptance of his own bad feelings will ultimately help him to cope better and enable him to love his siblings better (eventually, that is), you may find the strength to allow him to express difficult emotions. After all, it is the bad feelings that cause all the trouble. The good feelings take care of themselves.

The New Arrival

The parallel story can be used as early as two years of age. Usually before that time you do better in being direct and talking to your child in terms of what is happening to him now. If you come home with a new baby when your child is twenty-two months old, don't think he doesn't have strong feelings just because he doesn't have the words. Voice his feelings for him. "Sometimes when you see Mommy feed the baby, you wish you could be a baby." One mother served juice and crackers to her toddler when she breast-fed the newborn. In this way she was giving the older child as well as the infant a feeding that he loved, but she did so in a manner that was appropriate to his age.

In addition to actively responding to your child's need, you can use words to explain the act. Tell him why you are doing something. "You can have a snack, too. This is a hard time for you. You used to be the only one." This helps give even the very young toddler an understanding of what is happening. Perhaps it leaves memory traces in his head. These can be called upon at a later time when feelings bedevil him and he needs to sort them out for himself. In short, it promotes the development of insight.

The Middle Child

The middle child needs his own story. (He is in the middle whether he's smack in the middle, or second, third, fourth, or more.) The story can touch upon elements that are familiar to him. "There once was a little girl named Polly. She had an older brother and a very big sister. Her big brother played baseball a lot. Her sister was like Mommy. She took care of Polly sometimes, and she was even bossy." You can warm to the custom-made story with, "Polly did not like her big sister telling her what to do. She wanted to take care of the new baby herself."

Polly agrees vigorously. She has been a pretty bossy sister herself to the six-month old newcomer, Larry.

"It was hard to be in the middle. The big kids stayed up later and even babysat, and Larry was so cute, everyone paid so much attention to him." You can stay with the theme that those ahead of the middle child can do more things and have more privileges. You also express the pull of wanting to be a baby, since gratifications abound for the little one, and everyone responds to a baby. You can use the phrase "left-out feelings" to describe the state of the child in the story. Labeling feelings is the first step in their mastery.

Sometimes a child will recognize that you are talking directly to him. You can acknowledge his recognition.

He may prefer direct discussion, and it is easy enough to drop the story in that case. The main reason for employing the story is the greater neutrality it brings to highly charged topics. If he prefers to drop the pretense, do so.

You don't have to have an ending to these stories. Generally young children are so intent on hearing their feelings voiced they don't even notice the limitations of the plot. If you've acknowledged that it's a made-up story you can say, "We'll make up some more tomorrow." Maybe he'll give you ideas about how to proceed. If you've told the story as a genuine happening, stay with that. In all of these methods you are telling the child about himself and showing him respect for his many parts, the bad as well as the good. You help him like himself more as he accepts what he feels, *no matter in what direction it takes him.*

Thoughts Are Not Actions

This is where we differ from parents of an earlier age. The Victorians expected good behavior from their children. The "no-nos" were clear and the discipline (most often punishment) was exacting. That system led to difficulty because the feelings that precipitated the action were denied as well.

Children were told how they felt. And they were told they felt positively.

"We love one another."

"You love babies, don't you?"

For a child who felt otherwise, an inner split often occurred. He was cut off from part of himself. He by no means felt loving at all times, so self-criticism and self-loathing followed. He hated himself for his angry thoughts.

But thoughts are not actions, and this is an important distinction. It is important to get over our prejudice about them. Thoughts are of all kinds, hateful and nasty as well as loving and kind.

Acknowledging that thoughts exist is only the truth. The child is stronger for it and better integrated as a human being. As adults we don't remember all our negative childhood feelings because we have forgotten the earliest years; but if we know something of our own conflicting feelings, how much richer and wiser we are! Self-knowledge, even of the simple variety I am talking about here (such as jealousy of a sibling or the wish to be first), enables us to get a handle on ourselves, and we are able to behave better.

The story provides an outlet for the unacceptable side of human nature without allowing these feelings to be put into unacceptable action. It is a safe release for the child, as his feelings are accepted in a removed way. The story is about *his* feelings, but it is not only about him. Billy has the same feelings Eric does. Through a story a child learns that his feelings are okay, that indeed others have sad and angry feelings too. You need not scold a child for having bad thoughts, as parents did in an earlier time. Today we have a more balanced view of human nature that recognizes that wretched thoughts exist and that people are not evil for having them. Acting on them is another matter, however. You repeat, "You can feel and say it, but you can't do it."

Acknowledging the Good and the Bad

Are you being a hypocrite to acknowledge to each child that he has a unique position and a unique response to that position? No. Each child does have a special place. All you are doing is bearing witness to the right of the child to have his feelings (random, inconsistent, hostile, selfish, or whatever) accepted. These feelings change rapidly in the course of growing up. The child who hates a sibling today may love him tomorrow. The chances are better that this will happen if the nasty side is not denied.

But don't retreat from your own judgment of what

you expect in behavior. "Even though you are mad at Billy, you can't hurt him" has to be the repeated refrain. A reason is not the same as an excuse. For the younger child of two or two-and-a-half who needs physical release, a substitute punching bag can be provided. Words are not yet readily available to him. For the three- to five-year-old, however, words are more useful, and the story is a way of using words that apply directly to him.

The Victorian stance about feelings often led to hypocrisy because it denied the existence of negative feelings. If feelings were recognized, a moral judgment was passed on the sinner. Thoughts were confused with actions, and people were made to feel guilty for things they had never done. Wise children learned soon enough to simulate socially acceptable feelings, although this was not the same as actually feeling them.

Now you can have it both ways. You can help civilize your child in terms of graded expectation (much as the Victorians did), but you can also help the process along by an honest admission of the intermittently villainous feelings that beset everyone. You, too, pass a moral judgment. "Cruelty is bad," you say. But you make the distinction between feeling something and doing it. You acknowledge that the child may have a conflict but you expect him to do better. He learns to prefer the civilized way as you are consistent in expecting it of him. The parallel story, in effect, helps admit the inadmissible but does not permit the unpermissible.

He says, "I want it."
You say, "No."
He says, "It's mine."
You say, "Share."
The disagreement in these exchanges is unavoidable. There is a necessary conflict between infantile behavior and adult socialization. When you tell a story you soften the confrontation by your understanding. You say, "Ellen didn't want to share. She wanted to have the cake

all to herself. It was hard to give her friend a piece."
Ellen may agree with you on this. "But she did it," you
add. "It's not easy, but friends learn to share. Someday
Karen will give you a piece of cake when you want it."

Generalizing can be useful in a story. "Other little
boys and girls often feel this way." A child's self-esteem
takes less of a beating when he learns that others share
his plight.

A View of the Table

The story can be used in any number of life situations
that cause distress for children, including those that have
been discussed in the book as well as any unique ones of
your own. The parallel story allows the child to be the
judge and to see all sides of an issue. It gives him a view
of the table, which in his infancy he couldn't reach.
Sometimes he takes pleasure in the cruelty of a familiar
fairy tale in a book. Sometimes he enjoys the supermoral-
ity of a story in which only goodness and kindness pre-
vail. Learning that many feelings are allowable (if deeds
are not) increases maturity and self-control. The knowledge that you can feel two ways about someone—love
and hate are often close—and that the world doesn't
come to an end is a genuine comfort to a child.

You may be surprised at the depth of feeling your
child reveals in response to a story. It tells him how
much you understand him and how fully you accept
him. But don't expect to be appreciated every time you
tell the story. Sometimes it gets too close to the bone, and
the child tunes out. He doesn't want to understand what
you are saying. That's the time to stop. Don't ruin the
effectiveness of the parallel story by overdoing it.

9.
Temporary Separations

"**W**HEN you go away, Mommy, it's cold," says three-year-old Ruth Ann. "Don't go," she adds.

Not all children are able to express themselves so graphically, yet all children react to separation from loved ones, and the younger they are, the more anguish they feel. These are not separation problems. These are separation feelings, and they are perfectly normal. They never disappear entirely. Even adults show traces of them. Have you ever noticed your own letdown feeling when someone you care about takes a plane? Or the emptiness of the house when your husband is on a trip? It is painful to be separated from someone you love, and for the child under three it is practically unbearable. His relationship to you is his lifeline.

Your child develops physically and emotionally as a result of the bond you build by caring for him. It takes him months, in the beginning, to know you are you. At about seven or eight months old he shows very clearly that it is only you that he wants. When he develops locomotion, in the second year, he loves to get away from you—but not for long. And he doesn't like it one bit when you go away from him. This is one of the reasons that he keeps returning to check you out. He likes having Mommy near, even though he enjoys his independence and runs away from her at every chance. But don't confuse growing independence with lessening need.

Between eight and eighteen months he is particularly susceptible to your leaving him. "He won't let me out of his sight" is a frequent complaint. It is important to realize that these reactions are typical and that they occur less often as his ability to judge time improves. In the preverbal stage the child finds certain things more difficult, and separation is one of them. When he is able to voice his concern, as he starts to talk, and understand your words of reassurance, he learns that he needn't fear what is the basic concern of his young life—abandonment.

Keep Early Separations Brief

Because you are so central to the child's development before the age of two, it is best to keep early separations brief. An afternoon or an evening away is as much as he can tolerate, given the limitations of his small intellect and his all-important need for your presence. If you have left him for a longer interval and have had no problems with him as a result, it may be that he is one of those children with a greater ability to cope with strain. But you should recognize that your leaving does put pressure on him. The "go away but come back" concept isn't firm in his mind until almost the end of his second year. Your comings and goings teach him about it gradually. He may react strongly to even short separations. Such reactions are normal and to be expected because his concept of time is so poorly developed. Making friends with other mothers in similar circumstances can help you ease the bind of a child-centered world at this time.

Between the ages of two and three he can cope somewhat better, but he still does not respond well to your being away for more than two or three days at a time. Some mothers have assumed that by being away a lot they are training the child to accept their absence and helping to build his independence. But such an approach asks more of the very young child than he can handle. The steps to independence are gradual ones. You increase your expectations as he grows older.

Keeping separations short before age three may not always be possible. Perhaps you are having another baby, or must have an operation, or need to help your sister's family in a time of crisis. Vacations away from children are also imperative, and I would have tunnel vision indeed if I did not recognize that other factors play a part in a busy mother's life. For the time being, however, let's stay with the ideal (never realized by anyone, please understand) and recognize that if you must leave a young child, he will find it difficult to accept your absence.

For the working mother, other factors must be dealt with and in Chapter Sixteen, I address those issues. To keep the ideal in mind, however, should prove useful for those of you whose workday requires separation. It charts a course to steer by, even if the course itself proves difficult and uneven under current work schedules.

If You Must Get Away

If you need to get away with your husband for a child-free vacation (who doesn't need this at times?), it is better to take a number of short trips than to be away *once* for a long interval. A series of weekend overnights can relieve the tension for you and educate the very young to the reality of your return. Sometimes they are so dreadful when you return that you wonder if it was worth it. It is. For you it is a break in routine; for them it is a maturing experience.

One mother announced as she was leaving my office

that she was going on a trip in two days. "How shall I prepare my two-year-old?" she asked.

"Will you kill him if you don't go?" I asked.

"No question about it," she answered.

Not one to encourage infanticide, I helped her plan things in the time she had. All of us have to work within the limits of the possible. But knowing the ideal can help us plan when we have some control over choices. Between one-and-a-half and two-and-a-half the child may give you a hard time when you go, but he is better able to tolerate your going than the younger child.

If you must leave, speak to your child beforehand. If he's still in the preverbal stage, talk anyway. Talk as if he's five years old. As I mentioned before, his understanding outstrips his ability to talk. Leave something of yours with him when you go—an old sweater, a scarf, any belonging. This serves as a stand-in for your presence. For the older child, pictures are useful. A tape of your voice explaining where you are can be an aid. Having the babysitter talk about you while you are away is also fine.

One sitter drew a map of the place Mother and Father were going. She had blown up eight balloons for the eight days they would be away. Each day she had Margaret and Teddy break one balloon, and this seemed to help them understand the time concept. Crossing days off on a calendar is another way of helping children recognize that time does move.

The First Vacation

After the age of three a child can tolerate a separation of a week more easily. You can now plan a vacation and talk about it ahead of time with your child. Parents often hate to do this because it is like asking for a thunderstorm. The child becomes angry or tearful or pleading—"Why can't I go?"—and the joy of getting away diminishes with each scene. What you'd like to do is sneak away or tell him at bedtime that you are leaving the very next morning. The same desire for peace at any price lies behind telling the child who is going in for a tonsillectomy that he is going to a "nice place where you will eat ice cream." You want to escape his wrath and sorrow.

This is one time when genuine courage on your part is required. The sooner you tell him the facts and allow him to feel his distress, the better he will be able to manage while you are gone. In this sense, bad is good. In the long run you will find that his independence has been strengthened by your effort to help him meet a difficult event. By giving him a chance to antici-pate the separation, you allow him to deal with the fact of your leaving, the feelings that come as he anticipates it, and finally the fact that you will be coming back. That he is upset before you leave in no way means he will not be able to cope; in fact, the opposite is true. When you let him air the sad, angry, or fearful feelings while you are there, he has the comfort of your under-standing and explaining. This stands him in good stead when you are not there. "Mommy come back. It's okay," said two-year-old Roger as he patted his own hand.

This bubbling up of feeling at a time of separation is all to the good, although it can be very hard for a parent to take. Your goal, in helping him face a painful situation such as a good-bye from a loved one, is to allow his distressed feelings expression.

Children under five are given to emotion of great depth, and while it is true that parental expectation leads to good behavior, it is also true that allowing painful feelings to be expressed makes for a more genuine ac-commodation in time. It is better for him that you hear his crying and witness his bad tempers. It is not pleasant, but it builds toward a later serenity. It also builds a trust in you. Over the years he knows you are to be counted on to understand him.

Mastering Separation

An increase in your expectation that he can manage apart from you for longer intervals recognizes the contribution of maturation. That is to say, as he gets older he can deal with your absence more easily. As he understands more and is able to do some things for himself, he is better able to cope with your demands. He doesn't feel so helpless in the face of what he regards as your desertion.

One two-and-a-half-year-old became very balky when his mother left him for a series of afternoon appointments. She took up with him the fact that he was angry. (He'd had a tantrum and smashed a toy.) It was hard to be left behind. The next time she left him he announced, "And now *I* go bye-bye!" He had seized his coat and was halfway out the door before she could stop him. He glared at her for the interference. "I go," he said emphatically. "You stay. I go bye-bye. You stay home." A moment later he returned and patted her hand. "Mommy feel bad. Okay, Mommy." He had turned the tables on her neatly and was doing to her *actively* what he had experienced passively.

This is quite an advance in emotional mastery. It lies behind many pediatricians' recommendations that young children be encouraged to give their dolls shots after a doctor's visit. It turns the situation around and lets the children be the active inflicters of pain rather than the helpless receivers. It defuses a lot of anger that normally is aroused when a person is helpless in the face of pain—and separation is pain.

Mastery of separation is better handled on a piecemeal basis. Each time you leave he learns more about the world of reality. Once again you tell him the facts. "I have to leave." Don't deny it or sneak out to avoid a stormy scene. Prepare him early enough so he can deal with the feeling *before* you go. When you finally have to go—go! If you have fudged it in the past, admit now that that was a mistake and tell him you think it important that he know what is what.

Babysitters

Certainly mothers need time away from their children if they are to keep their sanity. The importance of having a reliable sitter (whether a neighbor, a student, or a relative) cannot be overstressed. It helps the child tremendously if the same person is there each time you go away. The child then begins to relate to that person, and the constancy of the same person helps him adapt more successfully. It may not be easy to find a steady sitter in our mobile age. But it can be done if you recognize its importance. Look for someone who is friendly, competent, and *there.* If you need to use a sitter he doesn't know, have the sitter visit your home beforehand to get acquainted. A babysitting session is practice for him. Again I am speaking of the ideal. When circumstances are less than ideal, be prepared to pay the price. In clinging. In talking. In working him back to his former security. Keeping children together rather than farming them out individually is very helpful. Older siblings help little ones a great deal.

Pools of young mothers for children under three, though handy and inexpensive, often make things harder for toddlers. The kids have to relate to too many people, and often normal separation feelings get lost in the shuffle. If you are in a pool, try to limit the reciprocal sharing to *one* friend. There's less stress for him in that.

Nursery Schools

If you enroll your three-year-old in a nursery school, or its improvised equivalent, you should arrange to stay with him at school for a week. Three days may be sufficient, but more is better if it is at all possible. Sometimes several weeks are required, and occasionally even more time is necessary. If your school discourages parental involvement (even good ones have been known to send a bus), try to persuade the teachers to let the separation process happen. You can ask to sit in an outer office. Your child can be given permission to run out to see you at times when he needs to check. Talk with him at home each day about the fact that you are reducing the time you spend at school the next day. This gives him a chance to cope with his feelings. At three it's better if you can take your child to school in the beginning. Car pools and buses are more acceptable to him at four. Here again it is a gradual process.

A child feels three sorts of emotions during a separation from parents—sadness, anger, and fear. You may see all, one, or none of these as he struggles to adapt to new conditions. Often it may not be clear that he is reacting to a separation at all. He may act as if he is angry at something else or sad about an entirely different issue. Or he may show no overt response, as was true with four-year-old Kathleen.

On Kathy's first day at school she haunted the front window of the nursery, searching for her mother. At the close of school, when she saw her mother walking up the path, she turned her back on her and nonchalantly began to paint. Her mother's face, bright with expectation when she arrived, fell. "She's so indifferent," she said to the teacher. "She didn't miss me at all."

Parting Is Not Sweet Sorrow

Regardless of what you see, sadness and anger about separation are normal. Parting is not such sweet sorrow for the very young child. You've caused him pain so he is resentful. Fear may not be present, but if it is, it may be disguised. You may see a stirring up of fears at night (remember, bedtime is separation too) as a reaction to his separation from you during the day. If he wants bad things to happen to you because you left him (tit for tat is characteristic of the thinking of children under five), he may then be afraid that they will. His love for you activates concern for your welfare, and often a temporary clinging is noticeable at separation time. By handling separations in a slow and gradual fashion, you will find that these feelings lessen. Once again, talk is the most helpful way to make this happen.

Four-year-old Nancy was told she had to go to nursery school because her parents thought it was good for her. This was a sensible decision on their part. What made Nancy more agreeable to the plan was their talking to her about her feelings of strangeness at school. They had moved from another city six months before. Now they talked about her old friends and how much she missed them. She was lively at this point and warmed to the subject. She missed her friends. She hated the new town. Why had they moved? She cried about the old house; she liked her wallpaper in that house better. Her parents acknowledged how hard all this was. They said it would take time to get used to the new school. But then when they insisted she comply, she went easily and the adaptation process was under way.

Once more, the point is that there are *always* feelings about separation. When we don't see or hear about them it is because we haven't given them a chance to surface. Children clue in very fast to what's tolerable for us and what isn't. If you can talk to them honestly ahead of time, allow them to express their feelings in words, and then leave as planned (I recognize that the problem may then be to enjoy yourself), you will have given them a chance to master the most basic infantile anxiety.

In a way, dealing with the separation feelings of little ones is like writing a term paper. In preparing a term paper, you first state what you are going to do. Then you do it. Then you describe what you did. Introduction.

Body. Conclusion. There is a similiar approach to dealing with separation:
1. You tell your child what is going to happen.
2. It happens.
3. You talk to him about what happened.

Sudden Separations

There are times when emergencies make it impossible to follow these recommendations. Nevertheless, there are still things that can be done. If you go into labor in the middle of the night, wake your toddler and tell him you're going. Call him on the telephone the next day. Send a toy or hospital trinket via Daddy. Supply the sitter with some small toys (one for each day) to give him from you. This much can be planned in advance. Keep communication open. He may retaliate and ignore you when you return. If so, talk about that. Talk about his disappointment, his missing you. You may need to provide the words for him, but you can be sure he will be listening intently and be relieved at being understood.

If an even greater emergency arises and you are unable to prepare your child, have someone else do it. Fathers —or sensitive neighbors or friends—come in handy at times like these. They can help the child to talk over his feelings about your sudden departure.

He may cling for a while after a surprise separation. You may find this very annoying, particularly if he is four or five and seemed beyond the clinging stage when you left. But he needs to do this. Here again talk is helpful. He might need a night-light, just as if he were a baby again. That is okay, but *don't* lie in bed with him or be a prisoner to his every whim. Try not to let guilt make you a victim of infantile tyranny. *Do* recognize fear when you see it and slowly wean him back to his former level of maturity. You may need to sit near the door of his room at night if irrational fears spring up. Recognize, however, that they are temporary and reduce the time you give to this each day. It is a way of unrolling worry backward.

It is useful to hold up the goal of managing by encouraging his feelings *first*. "You used to be okay about Mommy's going." He still clings to your skirts. "But then I went away for a long time." (Three days to the toddler feels like three years.) He holds tighter. "Now you're afraid I won't come back." He nods vigorously. "But I will." If an impasse such as this has developed, make your first absence after the separation brief—say, a half hour. The second absence, an hour. Work up to an afternoon. His irrational anxiety will diminish with each return.

Concise language is useful.

"Mommy goes away."

"Mommy comes back."

For the preverbal child, it helps to keep him in his own home when you leave because it is familiar and therefore feels safe. It is better to have Grandmother come stay at your house than to drop him at hers, unless, of course, he is there frequently and knows it well. Children feel separation from their homes very acutely.

On one family vacation the parents took everyone along. Alec, who was two, complained constantly. "I miss my upstairs and my downstairs," he said. Here he was missing *place,* not people. But these complaints, though valid for him at this age, were trivial. Everyone had a good time, including Alec.

Children of three and four take all of this better. Their time concepts are clearer and they can do many things themselves.

Moving

Moving to a new house may prove to be a genuine hardship for children of any age. Here again, talking about it ahead of time and allowing normal negative feelings to be expressed make the final moving day easier. Some parents take pictures of the old house before they leave. Describing the new house can also be useful. One mother bought play furniture and a toy van to help relieve her three-year-old's anxiety about the move. Any realistic preparation you do pays off by strengthening your child's ability to cope. Rehearsal is the name of the game. Here again, you are assisting the child's maturing. Don't be surprised, however, to find that more talk will be required after the move, no matter how well you have prepared for it. The child will complain about changes anyway—simply because he likes things that are familiar. Time is on your side as he slowly makes new friends and begins to be part of the new community.

Talking about painful feelings with children, particularly when you cannot alter a fact, is not easy. Most of us were raised with such time-honored adages as "Let sleeping dogs lie" and "Don't cry over spilled milk." The idea that ventilating feelings can help the coping process is a new one for most of us. Yet, if we stop to think of situations in our own lives where we were allowed to express our feelings in an honest way, we will gain some appreciation of what a relief such candor offers to the young child.

10.
Large Separations: Death

*M*ost separations are controllable. You have the final say on when you will be leaving, when you will be coming back, and where your children will be staying while you are gone. Even small separations require special handling, but generally they are manageable once you accept the fact that your absence is significant to your child.

There are separations, however, that are not controllable, and both you and your child must struggle with the helpless feelings they evoke. Death is the most difficult of all these. It is final, and it is a permanent loss. There are no concrete, satisfying answers to why a person dies. The way we respond depends on our own life history. We may respond in ways we could not have predicted, for every time death strikes someone close to us, it is new —even if we have dealt with death many times in the past. Death is always new. The person lost has never gone forever before.

Here is a place where our intellect tries to serve us. We know and have known for many years that all living things die. Man is part of this cycle. We acknowledge the inevitability of death when we attend a funeral, pay a tribute to a friend, visit a widow or widower. But even as we do this, we want to rush past. We mourn our own loss in the person gone, and often we find his family's grief too painful to witness. These times remind us most poignantly of our own mortality.

What is strange is that each time a loved one dies, it comes as a shock; death seems an invader. It is as if our intellect knows something that our feelings reject. Almost all of us live as if death will not happen to us or our loved ones, as if death is something that happens to other people. Although we know the facts with our minds, we reject them with our hearts. In that way, we are able to function well on a daily basis and live as if there were no end to the tomorrows.

When loss comes, adults lose the sense of control that sustains them in their daily lives; they feel helpless. It is therefore much harder to deal with your children's loss when you are trying to cope with your own.

It might not be possible. If the person who died was very close to you, you may not be able to help your children very much at all. Facing your own feelings may be all that you have the emotional energy for. You will be embarked on a long process of feeling your sorrow over and over. The feelings death brings are complex and varied. You may feel sorrow at one time, remorse at another. You may be irrationally angry at the person who died. (It was his leaving that caused you the pain, wasn't it?) You can feel relief that the person's anguish may be over. Guilt may follow, or depression—a feeling that life isn't worth living without the other person. Sometimes a forced gaiety ensues.

So you are busy emotionally, not just for the week or two when people pay calls, but for months and possibly for years.

In the real world of action, however, what you do is *do and make do*. You struggle to adapt, and what aides you most at this difficult time is your fundamental resilience.

"Who Will Take Care of Me?"

Where children differ from adults in this regard is in their immaturity. They, too, have profound feelings of loss; they, too, share in the bewilderment that confronts all of us at a time when no earthly claim can make a difference. But they are children. And what characterizes the child (particularly the very young child) is his absorption in himself. What matters most for him is how the loss relates to him and to his needs. If the person who died was his caretaker (mother or substitute mother), his first need is to be assured that someone will take care of him. Often he will not be able to express his sorrow until he has a relationship with the new person. He has to have continuity before the trauma can be dealt with.

"Who will take care of me?" asked four-year-old Kevin when his mother died. When an aunt stepped in and assumed his daily care, then and only then could he miss his mother. A child of five, when told of her mother's death, attached herself to the minister's wife and could make no reference to her loss until she established a permanent relationship with a cousin who came forward. She had to reestablish the lifelines before she could let herself feel. Sometimes we mistake children's lack of demonstrable sorrow as an absence of feeling. We think they are callous or too young to realize the finality of death.

As adults we are reluctant to see children suffer pain. We often try to put a good face on things. "Grandpa is up in heaven. He is happy there." We want to soften the blow because we recognize their immaturity and comprehend that their understanding is limited.

Yet the explanations we give can never be really adequate, because no one knows for sure when abstract thought takes place in a child's mind. The child tends to think concretely. When we tell him about heaven he wants to know where it is; he knows what he can see, and if it's up in the sky, how did Grandpa get there? Still, if your religion includes belief in an afterlife and you can talk of it with conviction, it may help soothe the desperate, once-and-for-all feeling death brings to everyone. If you do not believe in an afterlife, acknowledging you don't know everything may allow the child to invent stories that serve him temporarily. Tell the truth as you see it is best.

Certainly how the child views death depends on many factors—his age, who the lost person was, whether the person suffered sudden or lingering death, whether or not the child witnessed the dying. All these affect him in different ways, and over a period of time his views of the event will change and change again. As his intelligence grows, he can take in the facts better. As with everything else, the questions he asks can be dealt with over and over.

Stating the Facts

Just what are these facts that need statement? The facts are what we on earth know with our senses. For the child under four, the major points are that the person died and can't come back.

"He wants to," said the mother of a three-year-old who lost his father. "He wants to but he can't." The child's feelings of loss surfaced as others "came back" but not his father. Slowly and over a period of time other realistic elements may be added.

"His body is in a box. No, he isn't sleeping. No, he doesn't get hungry or need clothes. No, he has no pain. He is in the ground. Yes, we miss him very much."

In your own words you state the following facts as the child asks about them. You don't give it to him all at once:

1. The person died.
2. He stopped living and breathing. He can't feel, or talk or be the way we knew him.
3. He is buried in the ground. Nothing can hurt him.
4. He isn't coming back.
5. We are sad because we miss him. We miss all the things we shared with him.

This last point is made with each of the others. Separation is the essential message for the younger child. He learns, as we all do, by the absence of the person.

Grief is of course a private matter, and the public demonstration of it may tell little of one's relationship to the person gone. But it is helpful not to hide your sadness from your children. A stiff upper lip may be admirable for your life in the outside world, but sorrow is real. Certainly in the privacy of your home, it should be expressed. Tears may not be your style, but if they are, let them fall. Tell the child why you are crying. It shows him that being in touch with feelings is human and not shameful. Sorrow should not be simply tolerated; it should be seen as something of value. If tight-lipped silence is your style, let him know verbally that you are sad. Tell him it takes time to get over feeling awful.

"No, I am not angry."

"Yes, I still love you even though I look upset. It is just that I am missing Uncle Bill."

Sometimes children find it hard to accept your sorrow. "Stop crying!" ordered Peter. He didn't want to be upset. Later he brought his mother a tissue. "That's for when you feel sad about Daddy."

One little girl whose brother was killed in a car crash told me she wished she was the one who had died. I asked why.

"They don't talk to me," she said of her parents. "My

mother just sits and looks out the window. They don't care about me! All they care about is him!"

Her parents had no idea that she felt this way. Their own loss was so overwhelming that they were barely in touch with her. Talk would have helped in this case. Even though nothing can be changed realistically by talking, there is relief in knowing that it is okay to feel. Sometimes feelings of sorrow need to be voiced many times. The more sensitive members of the clergy are aware of this when they visit a bereaved family, not only formally one or two times after the loss, but informally many months later. Grief is felt for a long time.

When you cannot manage to talk to the children because of your own misery, ask family members or close friends to do it for you. They are not as emotionally involved as you are; they can tell the children the facts and can help them during the crisis. They can be available for answering any questions the children may have. Delegating the talking responsibility can relieve you of a difficult task at a time when you are least equipped to do it.

Even two-to-three-year-olds can understand something of the facts they are given. Many have buried a turtle or seen a dead bird. The adult can relate to their experience if he knows of it. But even if they don't grasp what you are saying now, they know you will answer their questions, and as they comprehend more they can refer back to these talks.

Frequently grief is disguised in strange ways. Christine was mean to everyone at nursery school after her father died. She fought on every occasion, seeming to want to control the other children by her bossiness. Her inability to control the situation of loss—to turn it around and make it not have happened—made her want to control everything else. Her nursery school teacher said, "One of these days when Chris can talk about how bad she feels, some of this argumentative behavior will subside." Indeed, often children act mad as well as bossy. Sometimes they *are* mad because anything painful can inspire anger.

In mourning, some children regress. The last step taken in development is the first to go. If they recently toilet-trained, they may start soiling. If they just started nursery school, they may cling and clutch. Baby talk may recur. Sometimes silliness is observed. One family thought its five-year-old was unfeeling because he clowned at the funeral of his grandmother. "I was trying to make everyone happy," he said. "They all looked so sad."

Allaying Anxiety

Sometimes after a loss children become preoccupied with illness and dying. This is not morbidity but genuine concern. It is one of the reasons I stress honesty in giving the facts. You (or the person delegated to do this) cannot begin to help any child cope with his anxieties if he hasn't been told the truth. If you see anxiety about minor illnesses and small separations, talk to the worry behind it.

"What do you think will happen?"

"Mary says everybody dies. Will I?"

"No, you are not going to die. This happens when people are much older."

"Will Grandpa die?"

"Someday, but not now."

He may confound you with knowledge about a young person's death. "How come Johnny died?" he asks. Here you weave both comfort and fact into your answer.

"That was an accident. It doesn't happen very often. He had a special sickness."

"Did he get a cold?"

"No, it did not come from a cold or chicken pox. Your sickness is not the same. Johnny had a bad kind that didn't get better. Your sickness gets better."

"Are you sick?"

"No. I will be with you for a long time."

It may seem contradictory to you to tell your child that death comes only to older people. After all, that is not strictly true—young people do die. However, a young child relates the death of a young person to himself, and he has no way of knowing that this is a rare occurrence and not the normal course of things.

You will see children play games sometimes or talk among themselves (often wildly inaccurately despite your efforts to deliver the facts). Don't interfere at the time. Such talk is a way of working things out. Your honesty when they bring questions to you will enable them to see you as a reference point and to come back to you as their comprehension grows.

Growing up implies an ability to see things realistically. Your aim, as my recommendations make clear, is to allow this growing up to occur.

For the most part, children's grief over death (and much of our own) is like the feelings that surround separation. Since no one knows at what age children actually comprehend what death means, it is largely to these feelings that you direct your attention.

"I hate it because it's for always," said six-year-old Susan about the loss of her grandfather.

"When is Grandpa coming back?" asked her sister, age four.

In the first statement there is despair at the finality of death; in the second, the desire for reversibility. Your response is that you know they miss him. It is hard. This reaches to their sorrow about separation. Your understanding is comforting, even though it doesn't alter the facts.

Relieving Guilt

The younger the child, the fuzzier his time concept. But as he grows and recognizes the separation as permanent, he comes to deal with it in his own way. What you do is serve as a fact reminder and feeling comforter.

You may have to make clear to him that his wishes did not make this sad thing happen. The child under five is given to the kind of magical thinking that assumes that thoughts are as powerful as actions.

"No, cousin Harriet did not die because you were angry at her. Thoughts can't make things happen."

Children tend to blame themselves for such painful events as hospitalization, divorce, illness, and death.

"If only I'd worn my boots like Daddy told me to," sobbed Martin when hearing of his father's surgery.

Cause and effect are unclear to young children. Children project themselves into conflicts as they try to understand why things happen.

"I should have been nicer to Edna."

"Robby got sick because I punched him."

This kind of thinking is at the heart of our own superstitions. We don't believe black cats are bad luck, but we'll cross the street to avoid one—just in case.

When young children struggle with causation, they tend to personalize. You may have to tell them again and again that one event had nothing to do with another. By being realistic you help their anxiety significantly.

Families must deal with death in accordance with their own customs, religious beliefs, and preferences. My own view is that a child under five is better off excluded from the funeral service. It may be too much for him to take in. Talking with him afterward may be more to the point. If you decide to take the young child to the service because you do not wish to exclude him from the family's solidarity, be sure to prepare him for what he will hear and allow him to ask questions afterward. If he questions what the clergyman says, you can express your own agreement or disagreement. It is all right to say that nobody knows for sure. I don't think viewing the body helps the very young understand death better; in fact, it may be more than the young intellect can assimilate.

It is better for the family to remain in the same house after a death than to make a precipitous move. In this way, the child doesn't lose everything—place as well as person. If you must move, talk about it and be prepared for the "looking back" feelings that such a move will bring.

If a young child witnesses some particular horror surrounding a death, such as a brutal accident or murder, it is important to seek professional help. Talking to a social worker from a children's agency or to a child psychiatrist or psychologist will give the child a chance to express his emotions and to deal with them realistically. This is really a mental health measure that can help to prevent future emotional problems.

Assuring the young child that he is still safe and that he will still be cared for is the most crucial aspect to handling death. His concern for self is central in the first five years. Your task is to help him feel protected in the face of frightening loss.

11.
Hospitalization

SOME philosopher has been quoted as saying that he couldn't be a philosopher when his toe hurt. Right. None of us is very philosophical about pain, particularly our own. The world looks very lopsided when we hurt, and going into a hospital hurts, whether we are in pain or not. Anticipating injury makes us anxious even if the aim is to make us feel better.

For the child under five, this is especially true. Hospitalization is a frightening experience. There is the strangeness of a new place to contend with. There is the separation from the people he counts on most. The young patient may be in pain from the illness or injury that causes him to be hospitalized. What further complicates the situation is that his concerns about himself often bear little relation to the severity of the situation. An earache that subsides with a shot is hardly in the same category as an ear problem that requires surgery. A broken leg in a cast is not an amputation. The child himself is often not able to make these distinctions. Thesi Bergman and Anna Freud, in their

Hospitalization

book *Children in the Hospital** make this important point. The loss of a tooth to a very young child may be the same as the loss of an eye. This accounts for the overreaction young children may have to very minor procedures.

Tell Him the Truth

Your first job then, when he is facing hospitalization, will be to make these distinctions for him. This will necessitate your knowing the facts, not merely what his hospital stay will mean in terms of his future health, but also what specifically is going to happen. He needs to be told why he is going to the hospital and what will be done to him when he gets there.

Getting the facts is not always easy. Doctors and nurses are busy people; they are bombarded daily with trauma and tragedy. Thus the request for specific information, particularly information of a routine sort, may seem unimportant and time-wasting to them. But the child under five does not really understand these distinctions, and it is important that you get as much specific information as you can about what is going to happen to him. In effect, you become a liaison between the staff and your child. Of course, it may not be fun to be placed in that position, but it helps him and that is the issue.

Your own feelings of helplessness and worry will need to be dealt with if you are to serve your child. Getting the facts straight from the doctor helps you too.

The steps involved in preparing a child for hospitalization are the same as those for separation: tell him what is coming, help him cope as it happens, and hear him out afterward. Responding to the questions that arise requires that you know the answers.

The child under three may have difficulty under-

---

*(New York: International University Press, 1966).

standing what will be done, but tell him anyhow. Unrolling the worry about the event will come later. Different procedures produce different anxieties, and you will have to modify your verbal preparation according to the situation that you face. If the hospital stay is elective, try to arrange a dry run ahead of time. Take him for a visit to the building. Show him what his hospital room will look like, let him meet at least some of the people who will be handling him, and tell him what will happen next. All these steps help to reduce unnecessary worry.

Stay Nearby

Whenever possible, try to stay with him. After five or six months of age the child is very much aware of your absence. Some hospitals have built adjoining rooms so that mothers can sleep in and be near their children. If your hospital does not have these modern rooming facilities, see if a cot can be put in his room. If not, curl up on a blanket on the floor. All young children benefit from having their mothers there, but for the child under three this is especially important. Separation in addition to pain is very hard for him to handle. If you cannot possibly be there, see if someone he knows and cares about can be near.

The young child's ability to judge time is poor, and even a brief illness can seem endless to him. You may be embarrassed if your child carries on, but try not to worry about it too much. Many of those who carry on are those who master the misery sooner. Since adaptation abilities vary in children, it is hard to predict what your child's reaction will be. However, the basic differences in children's reactions are those of degree, not kind. One of the most difficult things very young children face in the hospital is the loss of their own growing independence. The hospital makes them babies again, passively cared for; it helps if they can gripe about it, just as the chairman of the board might do under similar circumstances.

For emergency hospitalization there will not be time for preparation, but be sure to talk over your child's feelings about what happened after he's home. Children tend to think hospitalization is some kind of punishment for wrongdoing. If you listen to his play after he returns home, you may get some clues as to what he erroneously links together.

Relieve His Fears

Chuck, age four, in for a tonsillectomy, came out of surgery holding his genitals.

"I wasn't operated on," he said, pointing to his penis. "See?" This response came despite excellent preparation about what would be happening.

The worry about body damage seems to focus on the genitals after the toddler stage. As in sex education, if you ask him first what he thinks happened (his fantasies often reveal his worries), you will be better able to educate to the point of his concerns.

Since children are steadily moving through various phases of development, you can expect that whenever something upsets their inner balance (fairly unsteady anyhow), time will be required to right it.

Hospitalization is especially hard for the under-three-year-old. Tell him what is coming approximately two days ahead of the event. There are records as well as books available on the subject, and their neutrality can assist you in establishing your own self-control. When the big day comes, let him take along a favorite toy.

For the three-to-five-year-old, give about a week's preparation. Once again, as with all children, it is telling the facts that is important. Be brief and to the point. Try not to get into involved explanations. For example, regarding a tonsillectomy:

"You have to go to the hospital."

"The doctor is going to make you well."

"Yes, you will get a shot. But he will tell you when he is going to give it."

"Yes, it will hurt. He is going to cut out a piece of your tonsils that you don't need. But you will be asleep when he does it."

"When you wake up it will be over and the nurse will give you medicine to stop the hurting."

Don't avoid the hurting part. Most of us were told that we would be given a treat when we went into the hospital. Our parents didn't want us to know that any pain was involved.

Reactions will vary.

"I won't go!" said Larry. Talk revealed that he was afraid. "Who wouldn't be?" said his mother. "But you have to go anyhow."

Carol was serene. "I'm a big girl. It's okay." Afterward she cried. "If that's a hospital, I don't like it!"

Tommy covered his ears and started to sing loudly and gaily.

Prepare Him for the Unexpected

Even if you are as honest as you can be about what is to happen, you will still have to prepare him for the unexpected. Sometimes a child will see things in a way you couldn't have predicted. You may have to answer questions about the other children who are ill. Also, there are always unplanned things—the unexpected change of nurse, the intravenous shot that you did not anticipate.

It may help to state ahead of time that changes may take place. One mother said, "Sometimes something will happen that I don't know about now, but you can tell me about it if it happens." This helped her child to talk about the experience later.

The emphasis should be on the reality—who, what, when, where, and why. Allow for negative feelings, but don't let him wallow in them. After a time, be firm.

"But that's how it has to be." Always tell him when you are leaving. Always tell him when you will be back. If other family duties prevent your visiting as often as you would like or as often as you promised, be sure to call, even though you may feel hurt at the reception your thoughtfulness receives. Send a small gift. Keep in touch. Comfort comes in all sizes, and it's not spoiling to indulge a bit with extra treats. Hurts deserve some compensation.

You may hear from the nurses that your child behaves beautifully until you appear. He may start crying the minute he sees you. This is normal. He is only letting down after being good for strangers. It is a compliment, for he is safe in blaming his parents. They love him. He says, in effect, "How could you let them do this to me?"

Some hospitals employ staff members who devote themselves to helping children through the difficult emotional ordeal of hospitalization. These people are aware that a child may be tearful or fearful when he sees what is happening to other children. They see to it that a quiet place is provided for the child; they are available for explanation and calming down. No child under three can really understand why someone other than his mother should be caring for him. Thus the staff people who most often do this work (nurses, social workers, and child-care workers) often find themselves with angry patients. It takes a long time for trust to develop. With chronic patients, this is possible; with short-term patients, using mothers is often the best way. Here relaxed visiting rules help. When the needs of the whole child are understood, parents are not seen as interlopers.

Parents often learn a great deal about handling their children by observing the child-care staff in the hospital. Frequently such workers help the parents after the child leaves the hospital, not merely with the physical matters that need attention but also with the feelings involved. It is tacitly understood that the parents are important in what will follow at home.

When He Comes Home

Talk and more talk should be encouraged upon your child's return. It can take the form of play in which he works his feelings over. Sometimes he will be more direct. We all have a compulsion to relive something that is painful. It is a little like a splinter that must work its way to the surface. When the officer gave you a ticket for going thirty-seven in a thirty-five-mile zone you were properly meek. Then on the way home the dialogue with yourself began. You talked to yourself, you complained about the unfairness, and later you thought of the smart rejoinders you might have made.

A child's way of undoing something painful often takes the form of turning incidents around. If allowed to (at the hospital or at home), he now plays doctor. He gives shots to his dolls or stuffed toys. He yells orders and is very bossy and often mean (that's how it felt to him). This time he is the active perpetrator. Don't try to stop the play (as long as it's done to inanimate objects and not to children or animals). If he tries to operate on a sibling, tell him he can't. He can only play the game with toys. People have feelings.

"I have feelings," yelled Clyde, five. "The doctor hurt me!"

"That was to get you better."

"I didn't like it."

"Of course you didn't. He had to hurt you and that's no fun."

His anger is a healthy sign. He's working out an old grudge even as you do when you talk to yourself after something unpleasant. After a while the hurt loses its sting, and working it over and over helps to get rid of it for good.

You may see other signs of upset. Regression is one. Whining, thumbsucking, even wetting or soiling may occur. Encourage your child to put his complaints into words. Tell him you think he's having accidents because he's upset about what happened. If he doesn't respond to talk, make up a doctor or nurse game that includes his experiences. Generally he will become enthusiastic about this game, and as he becomes active, the more passive infantilisms will disappear. You can hold the line on his cleaning up his messes, but do make the connection for him.

By voicing his sadness, anger, or fear, or whatever emotion he appears to be contending with, you give him power to understand himself. So maturity is aided.

Although hospitalization can be traumatic for a child, it can aid growth—it can help cement the close relationship between parent and child as they work out hard things together. We have learned, in all these painful areas of real-life problems, that it is not what happened that really counts. It is how the person met and dealt with the problem that makes the difference.

12.
Fathers

FATHERHOOD changes a man's life. As one father said, "Children make a mess of your life, but somehow you kinda like it."

Most books on child raising emphasize the changes in a mother's life, but it is also true that a new father never comes home to the same life again. It isn't only that babies cry, take up room, and are expensive. Or that your wife seems to be listening with just half an ear, or that the house looks as if a madman was at it. It is that your life has been changed instantly and permanently. Someone has moved in for good.

Changes of Fatherhood

Luckily, many of the changes are positive ones. You become one of the two most important people in this new person's life. The toddler's leap into your arms when you come home at night can make up for a dozen sleepless nights. "That's my Daddy," from a three-year-old can cancel the choice expletives that came to mind when you stumbled over the tricycle left out on the walk.

In short, there are compensations for the long haul.

These are what parents remember fondly in later years. It is the short haul that may be hard, for fathers, too, are battling the nature of the child under five. They may be surprised to learn, as are their wives, that the ability to reason comes slowly to little children. Whatever theories about child rearing they held before, they are now faced with the practical reality of balky children who don't always behave as parents would like.

For fathers to know that this is the nature of children, and that it is not easy to rear social and considerate human beings from the tyrants toddlers are, is all to the good. It makes for a better understanding of the effort required to produce decent human beings. Some understanding of the irrational nature of the young (see Chapters Five, Six and Seven on discipline) can cut into the human tendency to blame the wife if the kids are bad. Children have a remarkable ability to stir you up and make you regress from adulthood. Fathers, like mothers, are not immune to the carrying-on of the under-five. You must work together with your wife or the kids will outflank, undermine, and overwhelm you.

The constant demands and messiness of the young child can be wearing on all who try to cope.

"I don't know how she stands it," one father confided. "Working at the office is child's play compared to child's play."

"I don't belong to the TGIF club any more," said another father. "I've joined the Thank God It's Monday group."

"I thought raising children would be a snap," said a third. "Now I think 'I'm okay, you're okay, they're not okay.'"

Father's Contribution to Identity

The issues involved in child care are, therefore, not simple ones.

Fathers, like mothers, are finding that being with

young children is difficult at times. When they actively pitch in to help they are not only easing the burden for their wives but learning a lot about the process of child-rearing itself. When parents can share their views with each other (each relieving the other when things get tough), family life is strengthened and children benefit enormously.

There is a renewed interest in fathers recently because of mothers' work outside the home. Some *are* taking a more active part in the daily care of their children. By and large, however, they are not, in great numbers, putting their careers on hold for the welfare of the children. This is what makes the issue of who will be caring for the preschooler such a big one today.

One father I know *is* staying home to care for his daughter as his wife remains on the job. He is enjoying his time with her enormously.

"Allison needed to be recognized as an individual. The group setting of the day-care center couldn't provide the attention she needed. At age three, she is thriving on the change we have made and my wife is less torn about leaving her with strangers."

Not every father can do this. "And," as one of the mothers I know added, "not every man is Alan Alda." Nevertheless, there are many families where parents share the care of their children, offering the kind of time with them that builds attachment and strong family feelings.

The mother's tie to the child is a biological one but, to quote Margaret Mead,* "the child's tie to the father is a social one." In general it takes time for Father to become enamored of a baby. (Childbirth classes and bonding opportunities at birth are helping to make this happen earlier.) This does not mean Father's tie to his child is less important. He brings his own uniqueness as a father

---

*Margaret Mead and Ken Hyman, *Family* (New York: Macmillan Co., 1971), 45.

and man to his role whatever he does in whichever way he contributes.

His sexual identity as a male is not lost because of this. Tenderness toward his wife and children are good qualities for children to witness. What is seen is respect for the other sex's contribution to the home. What you are in terms of gender and what you do are different things, and there is more freedom today to complement one another's role and still remain secure in one's own identity.

Children should be helped to be proud of what they *are*—girl *or* boy. An identification with their own sex yields self-esteem and something to aspire *toward* as they grow. In our zeal for equality today we have sometimes lost appreciation of difference as if acknowledging difference makes for acceptance of inequality. This will not happen if each sex is truly valued by both parents. The two-year-old particularly is sensitive to how these observed differences are fine tuned in terms of appreciation.

Recognition of whether he or she is a boy or girl develops at this time as similarities and differences are compared. Father as a model contributes to the sexual identity of the boy ("We are similar—you will grow up to be a man"). He contributes to the girl ("We are different but we complement one another"). The appreciation of either sex by the father is important to the developing identity of the child. To be like (for the son), to be liked (for the daughter) contributes to a sense of sexual identity, an important aspect of identity in general. Each family will find its own way in this regard. Children will identify with the qualities of the person they love even as they are clarifying who they are in terms of sexual identity.

Father and Intermittency of Contact

In some families the father is away frequently; in others he is on the scene almost constantly. Life's demands, career choices, and personal interests shape the time a

father spends with his children. For most fathers, intermittency is the name of the game, for even a job close by
requires comings and goings. Father's contribution to
the family is usually made in the time left over from his
work.

Intermittency has both its advantages and disadvan-
tages. In most homes the father works all day whether
the mother works or not. So he has a specialness for his
children just by virtue of his not being there constantly.
He can have a freshness of viewpoint, a perspective and
a resilience that only being away can bring. Children
look forward to their father's return and the reunion
may bring a special poignancy. Logjams can be broken
up by his coming home; he brings fun and diversion. Or,
if he so chooses, in his time at home he can do everything
mother does. He can feed, bathe, tell stories. He can help
in any way he sees necessary. But by virtue of the fact
that he is the one doing it, it becomes special. Often
rituals get established, since children like the security of
sameness.

"My Daddy reads that book to me. Don't touch it,"
said one little girl to her sitter.

"Daddy takes me upstairs," said a child to a visiting
aunt. "Then Mommy tucks me in." She added, "That's
the way we do things around here."

One disadvantage, however, is that the leaving and the
return may bring feelings of dislocation. A father may
leave a peaceful household in the morning only to come
home to one engaged in a war he knows nothing about.

"I feel as though I've come in in the middle of a movie.
It's hard to know what's happened," said one father.

"Shifting gears is rough," said another. "I've had pressure on the job all day. I'd like calm and quiet when I
come in. When the kids descend sometimes I feel as
though I'd like to hide."

"The kids' interests are so far from the work I'm
doing, it takes a leap of the imagination to take them

seriously," said a third. "I find it hard to be turned on by bubble gum."

Mothers have the benefits (and hardships) of continuity. For them the progress and steps of infancy, toddlerdom, and childhood bring advances that they are in touch with daily. Their need is often to break away. "Take me with you!" shouted one mother as her husband left for work.

"I'm stuck here all day," screams another in a famous cartoon caption, "and all you do is work in a nice cool sewer."

Reentry Problems

Reentry can bring its own kind of problem for Father. If a father has been on business trips a lot, guilt about his being away from the kids may make him a softie.

"What did you bring me?" demands Kathy as soon as he comes through the door.

There's nothing wrong with an occasional gift, particularly after a long absence, but you shouldn't make presents your means of pacifying your own conscience. If your work demands your being away, prepare the children honestly for your trips, write cards, even call. Keeping in touch is the most important factor, as children learn to accept the way your family has to live. The implication that you are making up for a defection is false, and you need not get into that kind of bind.

Because of the intermittent nature of most fathers' contacts with their children, the sharing of ideas between parents is extremely important. Mothers and fathers need to have the same information about what is going on at home. A father has to be involved in whatever concerns the raising of the children, whether it is toilet training, discipline, or study habits. When he and his wife reach agreement on their approach, he can then support it wholeheartedly. Parenthood is really a partnership in the fullest sense, no matter how often father is away, or for how long.

"If your husband doesn't back you up you can forget it," said one wife. It is as important, perhaps even more important, than his physical presence. Here quality time may be more important than quantity.

For the mother who is home full-time with preschoolers (with the possibility of regression around the corner almost a certainty), the importance of Father's emotional help cannot be overstated. She is deprived of the adult world she knew, and his understanding of this and willingness to step in as needed is of enormous support to her. It helps sustain the mothering process significantly, for if mothers are going to put their careers or interests on hold for the sake of good parenting, this effort of Father may be *his* most significant contribution of all.

The single parent attempting to do the job alone is undertaking something very difficult. (Parents Without Partners and other support groups testify to the need for the aid of others, and they are to be commended for the job they do.) Much can be done to help parents cope with such stressful circumstances. For example, other relatives can make a significant difference. Networking to find others to help can support the morale of a parent, and hence a child—not just in providing relief by babysitting, but by being part of the family's world. The old idea of extended family needs to be looked for among friends today.

When Father is away or out of town on business, reentry problems can surface. He can easily be put in the position of heavy.

"Wait 'till Daddy gets home!" shouts a mother whose patience is exhausted. Two energetic toddlers, being housebound by snow and measles, have reduced her to this weak demonstration of authority.

This practice is actually more common than not. Often mothers rely on fathers for the disciplining they've been threatening all day. In part this happens because mothers are there so constantly that children can easily tune them out. Mothers are also busy people and sometimes the chance for a confrontation disappears under the round of chores. Finally, mothers may be so fed up at the end of a day that they say, in effect, "Here, you handle these characters. I've had it!"

Presenting a United Front

Don't dodge the necessity to take a stand. Fathers play an important role in discipline because it becomes very clear after infancy that little children must be taught to behave better. Don't be afraid to exert your authority. Children need boundaries and feel safer when these are made clear. A child doesn't need a pal in you. He has plenty of those. He needs a father.

It works better when you and your wife take the time to discuss the children and figure out a strategy that works for both of you as well as for the kids. You double your strength by examining your assets and making them work for you.

One family I know was quite combative about its weaknesses. Mother was angry at Father because he couldn't bear to listen to feelings. She felt he was unsympathetic to her children's problems and insensitive to their emotional life. He felt she was a softie who couldn't make anything stick. Each felt wronged and compounded the problem by exaggerating what he or she felt was needed. Father came down more heavily on discipline "to make up for her." Mother listened to complaints more than was necessary because she felt no one else listened.

On the other hand, Father *was* sensible about discipline. Mother *was* able to hear. They turned it around. Weakness became asset when she supported his discipline and he encouraged the children to talk to their mother.

The children knew their parents' limitations. (Don't they all?) But they also received a united approach that helped everyone.

Children can create friction between parents. Try not to let them. The goal of viewing the children from a single vantage point takes some doing because you and your spouse came from different backgrounds and each of you can't help but respond differently to the various growth stages of your various offspring. Further, you are of different sexes, bore different positions in your own families, and had unique relationships with your own parents. All these play a part in determining your responses to your children. The effort to see the other's viewpoint isn't easy, but it can make an enormous difference in morale within a family. Whenever a father makes an effort to respect his wife's feelings about the children it enables her to cope better. And vice versa.

Finding Your Own Style

Martyrdom, however, isn't good for anybody. A father doesn't have to be involved in any way that is not natural for him. Trying to play ball with the kids if you hate sports won't work, either for you or for them. The real issue is developing an attitude of support and then finding your own comfortable style of participating. Like diplomacy or motherhood, fatherhood is the art of the possible. Knowing your own limitations can help you find compromises that are adequate for the family and bearable for you.

One father, determined to be an active participant in his children's life, began to hate Sundays. "He helps me with a vengeance," said his wife.

It may be better for the whole family to realize you need relief from your work and the kids as well, and that you need time for just yourself. The assumption that time with children is a rest for you may not always be true. This father did better on Sundays by allowing himself a tennis game in the morning. He then could really enjoy the children in the afternoon and was able to give his wife a respite. Trading off nights of sitting is another way to allow some time for each other's interests. There has to be a balancing of obligations so that adult needs are met too. You may have to plan ahead in order to find that balance. Too much sacrifice on your part can lead to the feeling that you should be rewarded. You may find yourself seeking good behavior from the children as payment for your own good behavior. This robs them and you of genuine independence.

Another father pointed to the condensed nature of his time with his kids. "Six to eight is the arsenic hour in my house. Everyone's hungry. The kids need baths. My wife is exhausted." After thinking it over, his wife changed her schedule. "I now feed the children before he gets home. Since I refuse to cook twice, he may get a twice-heated dinner, but we don't mind because the children are more amiable on full bellies. I also alternate nights for bathing the kids. They're a little dirtier and we're a lot happier."

It doesn't matter how you choose to cope with the abrasive times. Your choice is frequently a matter of custom and habit. But look for the problem areas and see if you can't make some simple changes. Full bellies before discussing *anything* of personal significance is not a bad idea for anyone at any age.

Other Roles of Father

In addition to being an authority figure, a father has a special significance for his children in that he is often able to play with them in ways a mother cannot. His fun is of a different order and sought by children all the more because it is unique. Often it may be whimsical or even downright silly but this can provide a break in the routine that is a release and pleasure for everybody.

"Carry me on your shoulders!" shouts Tom as Father walks in.

"Swing me!" begs Susie.

These are happy times for everyone and little need be said about them. Mother sometimes cautions against overstimulating the children before bedtime, and here compromises can be reached if the children are slow to settle in after too much physical play. For a father who enjoys sports the time will come when his children can share them with him. If you find that your children don't share your interests, try not to press them. Recreation pleasures vary and your children have a right to their preferences, as do you.

Father as Symbol

Sometimes a father becomes aware that he stirs feelings in his children that he did little realistically to inspire. These come by and large from the child's fundamental immaturity and his overriding need for protection. He will invent qualities in his father as his need for these is demonstrated. The qualities often change as his needs change.

"My Daddy can lick your Daddy," he shouts out of weakness and feelings of powerlessness.

"Daddy will fix it," he consoles himself when he breaks a toy.

"I want to marry my Daddy," says the little girl in her burgeoning femininity.

He can be seen as protector, authority figure, love object. He can be judge, policeman, caretaker. He can be ogre or helper, hated or admired. It helps for a father to know that he didn't do anything to account for these changeable, sometimes contradictory, and often intense feelings. These come out of the magical thinking of childhood.

Evidence of this appears with equal frequency in children whose fathers are permanently absent—through death, desertion, or divorce. These children, too, have strong feelings about their fathers, seen or unseen, remembered or not. These feelings may represent myth, fact, or fancy as the child develops. In such situations a mother may find that having pictures of Father about, talking about him or making some attempt at a link to him can help, for recognizing the importance of the symbol of Father contributes to a child's identity. Often in these circumstances a child chooses someone else who is close by to serve as a father figure. He will latch onto a neighbor, a friend, or an uncle, chosen on his own to meet his changing requirements. He may never verbalize his feelings or even understand them clearly but it's good to know that the meaning of Father need not be lost to him because his actual father is gone.

Father as Person

Of greater importance than the symbolic meaning of Father in a child's life is a father's realistic relationship with his children. Even the very young child relates largely to his parents on the basis of what they do for and with him. Function is the key word here. Children have attachments to both of their parents, and they respond to them in general in terms of how they are cared for. Children are concerned primarily with their own needs, and they view parental care in terms of how these needs are met. Here a father's realistic relationship with his children reflect his attitudes and qualities as a person. These vary from person to person, so what a father can be to a child will differ from one family to another. Even in families where the father is gone, and another man serves as father figure, the qualities of the person are what count.

Fathers also have an important role to play in the case of emergencies (when Mother or primary caregiver has to be away). If Father has not been too active in the care of the children before this time, the burden of primary care will tilt suddenly in his direction. He may feel over-whelmed at first, especially if no other help is available. The children need to be fed, bathed, disciplined, and comforted. Comfort in particular may be necessary be-cause they miss their mother. Following her routine as closely as possible will help them adjust to the change.

This is a good time to overlook some things that need doing in the house. If you're a tidy soul, your wife will appreciate the vacuuming and cleaning you do, but more than anything else she will appreciate your attention to the needs of the children. This is the time for shortcuts. TV dinners, peanut butter and jelly sandwiches, paper plates, and drip-dry clothes are fine. When friends invite you for a nice hot meal you may find that it's not as enjoyable a prospect as you thought. You have to get the children there. You have to get them home. Toilet train-ing and other more recently acquired skills may be shaky, and you may question the effort involved. If it's easier not to go, stay home. If well-meaning friends want to help, let them bring a hot dish in.

The children may be more demanding and more diffi-cult when Mother is away. Secure children often let the parent at home—you—have it, much as they let Mother have it when you are gone. The reverse may also occur, however. Children enjoy being with one parent, and a camaraderie develops in meeting a tough situation to-gether. This can make your relationship with your chil-dren stronger.

Talk about whatever is wrong in simple terms. Em-phasize the positive elements in the situation if you can, and count the days she'll be away. If the children are asleep when she comes home, wake them. For children as well as adults, being an active participant makes things easier to master.

Successful fathering, like successful mothering, puts you out of business. One father said, "I decided a long time ago that you can catch a fish for a child or you can give him a line." If you've determined to do the latter, your child will be on his way to an independence that serves him well.

The satisfactions that come to you as you watch your children's progress are intensely personal ones. These are not derived from the marketplace, for Father as a father is not defined by his children in terms of his success in the outside world. This is a comforting thought in these days of rapid change and social dislocation. Your family can reflect something of your own spirit, your own doing. Fathers can take pleasure in the power they have to forge a bond of identity with future generations.

13.
Sex Education

*E*VER since your child was conceived, you thought about how you would one day tell him how he came to be. You don't plan to repeat your parents' mistakes by hushing it up. You don't want him to think sex is dirty. You don't want him to rely on street information—or, more likely, misinformation. You want, in short, to do it right.

Cheer up. It's not that hard. What makes it seem so difficult is the fact that sex is a highly charged subject, even for the most liberated among us. We may know the end result we'd like to achieve—namely, children who accept themselves and their bodies and grow up to be the kinds of people who are able to have meaningful human relationships. But how to get there is the question.

As with other topics I've discussed, the educational process is gradual. Sex education requires that a child be aware of himself as a human being with ties to others, for no one conceives himself or develops independently of others. Man differs from many other species in this regard; he has a very long childhood in terms of being dependent on his parents for years. The child's knowledge of himself as a boy (or of herself as a girl) develops in the early years. Sex education involves helping the child to establish himself as a person and to build his capacity for mature relationships with others. It is not just teaching him the facts about where babies come from. If we tend to talk about birds or bees or pollen and get mystical about nature with our children, it is because this topic makes us nervous. Our zeal to get agricultural in our explanations or to align ourselves with others in the animal kingdom is proportionate, I think, to our discomfort in discussing these matters with children.

Sex Education Is Life Education

Sex education is really life education, and you have already done a good deal of it by the time your child is three years old. Whether or not you have used the methods in this book, you have done many things that helped establish your child as an individual. When you held him for feedings, when you walked him during illness, when you played peekaboo with him and enjoyed him in his bath, you were helping him take pleasure in you and in himself. His affection for you and yours for him build the very first tie in his young life. He loves Mommy in the beginning. His clinging and crying between eight and eighteen months is his way of saying he loves you. In effect, he says to strangers, "You are not Mommy, so get lost!" He is becoming selective in his choices; his ability to discriminate among adults who take care of him shows his increasing good sense. His preference for one person is a feature of loyalty. His undivided love for you helps build the ability to love the others who will eventually follow.

Toilet training, which all children eventually must undergo, contributes to body mastery and enhances the sense of self. While the methods recommended in this book increase the latter, it is also true that all children achieve cleanliness in time. This, plus disciplinary measures that help children achieve better self-control, are part and parcel of self-mastery, which is a natural precursor to relating to others. How much better you can like other people if you like yourself! Children like themselves better when they function well.

Teaching a child to be considerate is an important factor in sex education. When a father shares in some of the tasks of caring for house and children, a child learns a lot about how men and women relate to each other. Such gestures can demonstrate respect and add to a girl's pride in herself as a female and to a boy's understanding that a man can be sensitive and caring. It isn't only what you say. It's what you do. The parents' unity, often difficult to attain, particularly in the early years of marriage, is the best sex education of all.

Try to stand together on most things regarding child rearing, if you possibly can. Talking together at night can iron out a lot of differences. Most parents don't think of themselves as educators; but once they do and once they recognize how important it is for their children to see them in agreement, they find that, in matters of discipline especially, the effort is worthwhile. On the other hand, some differences are unavoidable. But from these, children learn another important fact: the world doesn't collapse because loved ones are angry with each other. Making up and forgiveness are part of living together. In this sense, sex education is a continuing part of your family life.

The Natural Approach

But the aspect of sex education that concerns modern parents most is how to make children comfortable with and unashamed of their own sexuality. The feeling among many parents these days is that what is natural should be accepted as natural. No one should feel guilty about normal body functions. The assumption here is that if these are accepted calmly from the beginning of life, the child will not regard them as dirty or as matters to be hidden. There is the conviction that one doesn't hide one's body; it, too, is a natural phenomenon. And since this seems a reasonable approach for us as adults, we tend to think it a good one for the children as well.

This approach assumes that input from the environment is the most significant factor in sex education. In effect, modern parents are saying, "See, we are not embarrassed. All is open here. You can see for yourself what sex differences are like." They assume that seeing is believing and, therefore, comprehending. The hope is that children, after seeing their parents and each other undressed, will ask questions that can be answered directly, without evasion. Then guilt, thought to have been inspired by the attitudes of a sexually inhibited society, will be eliminated. There is the hope that a better man will emerge from such honesty.

This type of thinking has developed as a reaction to the rigid, secretive view of sex held in the Victorian era, when sex was equated with original sin and repression was the order of the day. The modern recognition that all people have sexual feelings and that such feelings are normal is a significant one. Many proponents of the natural approach have gone further, however, concluding that man will accept his body functions with less self-consciousness if he is not constrained by a modesty that implies that enjoyment of physical pleasure should be hidden.

The Boomerang

The curious thing is that this thinking, which seems logical enough, has boomeranged in ways not anticipated by its advocates. Observers of young children who were raised with this open approach to sexuality found, much to their dismay, that the children were not freer because of the new freedom but instead were more excitable and often less educable. Four letter words, bathroom talk, much trying to see and touch seem to be a problem as never before in nursery and elementary schools. We are hearing more and more stories about sexual acting out on the part of children themselves. This has happened in part, I think, because while endorsing tolerant parental and societal attitudes toward sex many have not recognized the factor of infantile sexuality.

What we have learned through the close observation of young children over many years is that there are precursors to adult sexuality. Even very little children enjoy body excitements. They suck their thumbs or touch their genitals. Today this is viewed as normal, acceptable human behavior.

A long biological and emotional process starts when the child is born. In his early years the child has to contend with the physical excitements that erupt from time to time in normal development. What the proponents of the natural approach do not understand is that the child has his own feelings about body excitement. They are often surprised to learn that these feelings can lead to guilt spontaneously. Parental openness and nudity, rather than ridding the child of these feelings, frequently upset him. What we have learned in the study of young children is that it does not help the child to be put in the passive position of viewer. Exposure to adult nudity, with its size discrepancies, can be too much for the child when he is contending with dimly understood drives of his own. It is not a moral issue; rather it is one of overloading the circuit. It raises far more questions than it answers and mixes him up far more than straight talk that answers his questions.

A Practical Approach

This does not mean that I recommend a return to Victorian secretiveness and denial of sexuality. That period brought a suffocating air of hypocrisy to normal life.

Instead, I recommend that you talk to your child about what he wants to know. Talk is better than a demonstration, and it is sensible to make sex a permissable topic for discussion. In that way, you avoid the pitfall of the hush-hush school of thought as much as the problems of the exhibitionist school of thought.

Now, to be more specific, I recommend from the first, if possible (certainly by three months), having the child sleep in a separate bedroom. Even keeping his crib in your bedroom during the day (if space is limited) and rolling it into the living room at night is advantageous, because it announces firmly that sleep is sleep and that you and he both need some privacy in which to effect it. This avoids a lot of sleep problems later on and is worth the extra discomfort of making special arrangements. If there are older children who will be disturbed, it is still better, in the long run, that the baby share a room with them rather than with you.

I make a special point of this because there is nothing in the child's experience to explain what is happening in the other bed. He interprets what he sees or hears in the light of his poorly developed comprehension. Since infants cannot tell us their thoughts we generally only learn of their confusion later. What we have learned is that small minds misperceive and are often needlessly frightened. They take two and two and make seven.

One couple was horrified to see three-year-old Elizabeth next to their bed at night. "What are you doing to my mommy?" she asked indignantly of her father.

Stevie, four, told me his father hit his mother a lot when they went to sleep in his room. I asked why he didn't tell them it worried him. "Then he'd hit me," he said. The parents had assumed he had never observed them. "He's a sound sleeper," they said. This may make sense to you for your three- or four-year-old, but it is also true for the younger child. Even a child who doesn't have words can be frightened by what he does not understand.

This recommendation for privacy includes other areas as well—dressing, undressing, and toileting. You may be bewildered about this because so much of what you read advises otherwise. Further, you may wonder how you can follow this recommendation in the face of one bathroom and little ones tumbling over themselves to be near Mommy.

It is easier to do if you are first clear about the reasons. The major reason is that your child's mind is not able to take in realistically what he sees. He indulges in a kind of fairytale thinking at this stage of his life. Size differences loom as enormous.

"My father's pee-pee is one hundred feet long," Michael, three, announced to me sadly. His sense of proportion was quite absurd, but his outstretched arms, as he tried to show me the size, told me how he *felt* looking at his father—outclassed and inadequate. Even if a child doesn't voice his response, and most do not, it can leave him feeling unnecessarily "lesser than."

Learning from Peers

Feelings are attached to observations, and little ones do better when they learn about sex differences from their own age group. Size differences are then less of an issue. Even then, children under five have their difficulties. They assume, in the egocentricity of babyhood, that everyone is made as they are. When they are confronted with the reality of difference, little minds go to work and derive many elaborate, if false, conclusions.

"What happened to her wee-wee?" asked Johnny about a new baby sister. "If it can happen to her," Johnny added ominously, "it can happen to me." He barricaded his bed at night with every toy he could find, defending against a threat that was all in his head.

Amy, three, asked her mother matter-of-factly to put a penis on her Christmas list. "It's so handy for standing up," she said. She was very disappointed when she opened her packages that year.

This kind of "Anything I wish, I can make happen" thinking is very marked in the toddler. Here wishes come true, body parts vanish, and spiders eat little children. Avoiding exposure to the giants of his world eliminates a sizable hunk of unnecessary anxiety. By keeping your bathroom and bedroom door shut, you give the child a chance to cope, on his own terms, with his own biology. He doesn't have to deal with the stimulation that comes from viewing yours. He will still need to contend with the normal worries of his age, but they will not be so overpowering. And, as he grows older, his ability to understand will grow accordingly. Time is on your side.

Don't hesitate to answer if your child protests your shutting the door. "I want my privacy," you can say. Very soon he will demand the same for himself. "If you have questions, I'll answer them," you can add.

The Importance of Honesty

Your best bet in dealing with children's misconceptions is to be honest and to the point. Asking him what he has heard or thinks is a great help because then you can try to straighten out his distortions. It also gives you time to think of an appropriate answer. So ask him, "What do you think? What have you heard?"

You can tell Johnny that nothing has happened to his sister's wee-wee. Girls are made differently from boys. She does not have one like his but that is the way she is supposed to be. If you hear him make a remark that reveals a misconception, straighten him out on the spot; little children seem to require this. In each round with you, he learns a little more, and you don't have to do it all in one day. His intelligence is growing; a greater awareness is possible.

To childish minds, something visible is seen as a plus; something not seen is felt to be a minus. Both sexes struggle with the problem of difference and need repeated clarification. Michael needs to be told his fears are needless; Amy needs to know that she has something, too, but it can't be seen. It delights her to learn that she can have babies when she grows up. You can acknowledge that it's hard to wait till then. Two-to-three-year-olds, being in the "who's got what" stage of development, are inordinately curious, but this passes in time. It is succeeded by the "I want what the other fellow has" stage.

Richard, three-and-a-half, walked around with a peculiar gait as he stuck his stomach out ahead of him. "I can *too* have a baby," he stoutly maintained.

Little girls wish to be little boys; little boys wish to be little girls. They all wish they could be grownups and stay up later. It's a normal human belief that the grass on the other side is greener. In children's play we see a lot of switching back and forth; boys play with dolls, girls want to be daddies, and everyone likes to be boss. Mother wonders, as she hears her officious four-year-old telling off some younger playmate, whether she herself really sounds like that.

One of the nicest things about children's play is that it allows them to take any part they choose. They can always meet reality later with "It's only a game." But for the period of the play, children get a chance to express many wishes and ideas. You needn't interfere with ordinary play by stopping it and educating them. Play has educational and therapeutic advantages in itself. It is one of the means by which children learn to cope, and its variety and make-believe elements help children endure the painful swings of childhood. In play, they can make things come out as they wish.

Playing "Doctor"

However, when children want to examine each other or exhibit to each other, they should be stopped. This may seem like unnecessary adult interference to you, but "doctor" games and the like are not helpful to children because they are too stimulating. They can interfere with sleep, with quiet times, and with ordinary play. You can say, "I don't want you to play that. It's too exciting for you." Don't be afraid to break up group activities of this kind. You can say to them, "That's enough. It stirs you up too much." Stopping them is not what makes them feel guilty (which all of us agree we would like to minimize). Stopping these activities relieves children of spontaneous guilt by protecting them from doing that which is guilt producing—another real paradox in child rearing. Children are relieved when adults stop them, even though they may protest vehemently. If you insist on modesty for yourself, they will be less inclined to play these games, and their interest in them will diminish.

The Benefits of Modesty

Many modern parents have been used to undressing and dressing in front of their children. This does not mean that it is too late to make changes in the direction of more modesty; at any point you begin, your child will benefit.

David, five, was brought to me because of his out-of-control fighting in kindergarten. As I talked with him about what he thought his problem was all about, he announced, "I play nudies with my sister."

I asked, "And how do you do that?" To which he replied, "First we take off all our clothes except for our undershirts and underpants."

"And then what do you do?"

"Oh, and then we take those off." David's out-of-control behavior in school stemmed from his parents' genuine efforts to be modern and open about their bodies. When modesty was instituted, his behavior in school improved proportionately. Though not all out-of-control behavior has this source, reducing stimulation in the home decreases the chances of it.

Change Gradually

If you've let your kids wander in and out of the bathroom and bedroom at will, don't change your system abruptly. A sudden change in the rules may arouse more questions than it answers. If you see the point of this recommendation and are willing to go along with it, get into the change slowly. You might gradually introduce the idea of privacy and tell the children you prefer it. In a month or so they will probably be requesting it for themselves. If you feel you can't leave toddlers around to commit mayhem while you are in the bathroom, tie the baby to his dressing table and have the toddler wait on the couch or in the old playpen until you reappear. It may seem like an unnecessary to-do over a small matter, but the point is that it is not a small matter to them. They will stop trying to get into the bathroom after a week or so. If a child barges in unexpectedly, keep covered and tell him to leave. He'll catch on.

If you worry about his locking himself in, remove the bathroom lock and put up hooks both inside and outside near the top of the door to ensure privacy for yourself. He loves it when you respect his wish for privacy too, as when you knock before you enter. Obviously, with little ones who are toilet training, you will be in on their privacy for at least part of the training interval. Nevertheless, your requesting privacy for yourself sets a tone that is calming.

Sometimes parents are confused by the fact that their

children appear not to notice nudity and seem to take it in stride very well. There is no doubt that some children manage better than others, as some have a greater tolerance for excitement. But many children who seem overly aggressive are frequently working off sexual steam. Often this is not recognized by innocent parents such as David's.

You may feel that my suggestions smack of prudery and that children will become Peeping Toms if their view is blocked. This will not happen if you are frank in fulfilling their need for information. Their curiosity is real and needs an outlet. If they do play doctor, ask what it is they want to know. As in other areas of child rearing, such as discipline, you are saying "no" to the acting out of the curiosity and "yes" to the request for information.

Bathing Together

After they are two, I would begin to discourage bathing the children together. This too can roil them up and is really unnecessary. It doesn't mean becoming shocked and outraged if you find them looking or touching. It does mean stopping the activity in a firm way and then opening the way for talk. Recognize with them that they are curious and thereby show your willingness to respond to questions. This helps demonstrate your credibility and honesty. Later, when they have more pressing questions, it helps them to know they can turn to you. If separate baths are too much work for you, try bathing one child one night and another the next.

Family Ties

After the "I want what he or she has" phase, young children may show intense feelings of affection for various members of their immediate family. Between three-and-a-half and five, little boys want to marry their mothers, little girls their fathers. Sometimes boys want to marry their daddies and girls their mommies. They may love older siblings with an adoration that is quite unwarranted, since the sibling in question may pay absolutely no attention to this unsolicited hero worship.

A college student said to me, on hearing these theories about child development, "You don't have to do anything about it, right?"

Right.

The processes frequently go on silently, and you may never see or hear any of this. It isn't necessary that you do. Some children are more verbal than others; each child has his own style. The important thing is that you function as Mommy for them and that's real and safe. You are not actually a beautiful princess even though your son, at age four, may think you are. When four-year-old Lisa tells her mother, "I want to marry Daddy," Mother shouldn't feel offended or go into a long discourse on sex choices.

She can say matter of factly, "He's already married. You can't."

If Lisa then spends a year or two struggling with her frustration over this unavoidable fact, that's the way the process goes. Learning about reality takes time. There is bound to be frustration along the way. If Mother realizes that in a few years Lisa will want to do everything her mother does, she need not feel hurt by a preference her daughter is now so candid about. If Mother wants to, she can sympathize with the feeling. "It's hard to wait until you get your own husband." Sometimes a child's anger at her mother is a reflection of this normal phase of development. You don't have to get tense about it. Sometimes a child is irritable with one parent or the other for weeks, perhaps months, at a time. He may be going through such a phase.

One mother was always charming in her manner toward her four-year-old daughter.

"Good morning!" she said brightly as she entered her daughter's bedroom.

"It's not good!" said Margo balefully.

Mother threw open the curtains. "What a lovely day!" she continued in a vehemently cheerful tone.

"I hate it!" said Margo.

Mother felt like a failure. What had she done to deserve this? Not a thing. Her daughter was going through what might be called a developmental disease. Nothing Mother could do would please her because she saw her at this time in her life as her rival.

Once you realize that these feelings lie within the child and that they are transitory, you will be able to be more matter of fact and less hurt. When you know that it is *her* problem, you don't make it yours by trying harder to please her. You ignore some of her provocative testing, knowing that change for the better will come—eventually. She may want to fight about choice of clothes or other minutiae. These are transitory issues that you needn't get too involved in. They are times to be endured, and a rueful acceptance of a "You can't win" philosophy can help you survive.

Cooling It

The best way to deal with all these matters is to cool it. Modesty, privacy, and less roughhousing are all helpful. Try to separate the sexes, however difficult it may be. If a boy and girl must sleep in the same room, you can put up a screen between beds; even a blanket on a line will do. The children may evade you occasionally, but do send each back to his own side. By requiring privacy for yourself and expecting your children to respect the need for it among themselves, you let them know where you stand. Even if they circumvent you occasionally, it's a comfort for them to know you prefer less excitement, not more. It relieves them in the same way that all good disciplining does—by letting them know that someone will stop them from behaving inappropriately.

When you advocate privacy you are in turn, respecting *their* right to privacy. This can only be a help later to them as they have grown up with this attitude. If someone later invades their privacy (a growing concern in a time of worry about strangers), they are better able to see the intrusion as a "not right" thing. You have established your own family's "oughts and noughts," creating a protective shield for them in today's world.

The issue of TV can be a part of this problem for parents because a lot of programming features fairly explicit adult sex during the day. Many preschool children are tuned in to soap operas as their babysitters watch. Even good children's programming may be preceded by advertisements for movies that are violent and/or sexually provocative. A turn-off switch may be the answer at times. Some monitoring on your part of what is acceptable or what is not can certainly help. I don't think we can ever get the genie back in the bottle, but it is worthwhile finding out what is seen by your children. In this way you can hear from them how what they see is perceived by them.

Bed Problems

If you're short on space you may have to stagger bedtimes to maintain any privacy at all. Putting one child to bed in your room and then moving him later eliminates a lot of bedtime hijinks. It is best, if you can manage it, to have boys share one room and girls share another.

Letting children into the parents' bed in the morning is a common family custom that everyone enjoys. But it, too, may lead to unnecessary wildness. One mother I know who slept in the nude used to take her children into bed with her on Sunday mornings. One day her son, as he stood at the door, handed her a robe. "Is he telling me something?" she asked.

If Sunday morning pile-ins are too pleasant a family treat to give up, have the children play with toys on the floor near you or at the foot of your bed on top of the blankets. The cuddling that you enjoy in a maternal way may be misconstrued by the child when he's passing through a normal competitive phase at four or so. Please understand that I am not against all parental demonstrations of love and affection; they are as important to a child's development as the sun is to flowers. But warmth need not mean kisses on the mouth, and a cuddle need not mean breast fondling. Parental affection need not be seductive.

Toilet Training

Toilet training is a period where children often do a great deal of observing of each other. This is far better than observing adults, and I wouldn't make an issue of it. They can be allowed to talk about the differences as they observe them. If they seem to get too excited by such observations, tell them so and separate them. When they are two-and-a-half or three, you can press the need for privacy. Children often seem pleased with the idea of closing doors.

Masturbation

The calming environment you aim for should lessen a lot of infantile behavior. Masturbation in either sex may occur for a time; it is normal but it may need management if it becomes public. Tell your child that touching himself is a private matter. It doesn't belong in the living room. This acknowledges, in effect, that it goes on but defines it realistically as a private matter. No amount of saying "no" to a child about masturbation stops it anyhow. It is he who has to struggle with his thoughts about the rightness or wrongness of it, and he does better when we allow it to be his private business. The reason masturbation may become a kind of moral issue for *him* is *not* that we threaten him (days of predicting his genitals will fall off or that he will become an imbecile are gone forever, I hope). It may become one because, for the young child, masturbation often gets mixed with thoughts and fantasies of his own devising. (A sort of precursor of the adolescent years when concern about this issue is greatest.) Just remember: body interests are normal, generally silent, and you don't have to do anything about them.

Six-to-Ten-Year-Olds

At five and six the child becomes far more interested in others. Teachers become persons to admire; often parents count for less. The schoolchild turns more and more to friends and to learning outside the home, and others enrich his life as his world is enlarged. For a period of time his sexual interests become dormant. The elementary school child may show a casual interest in the opposite sex at times, but for the most part boys are busy playing with boys and girls prefer to play with girls.

This is the time of life when curiosity about the real world is at a peak. Children are eager to learn. They enjoy groups of various sorts and organize clubs of their own. These disband with great rapidity and new ones take their place. School-age children have private lives in which friends and secret exchanges are especially important. Camping may be a new interest for both sexes; collecting various kinds of objects can become a mania for a time. Music lessons, dancing classes, scouts, and a multitude of other special interests claim their attention. Your problem as the parent of an elementary school child may be to keep some free time open for him. For too many children of this age, the waking hours are overorganized. They need time to let their motors idle.

Questions about sexual matters come up occasionally in six-to-ten-year-olds but in a more perfunctory and academic way than they did when the children were under five and struggling for control. In a real sense, the subject gets easier. They have words to converse with, and they hear you in a new way. While they turn to friends for information (or misinformation), the fact that you have leveled with them all along makes them better able to judge and weigh what they hear realistically.

14.
More about Sex Education

MARK Twain's joke about the weather could be applied in reverse to the sex education of children: "Everybody does something about it but nobody talks about it." To which I would add, "And when they do, it generally mixes the children up even more." That is because no one really helped us to understand when we were young, and we find ourselves tongue-tied as we try to explain emotions and experiences that are really nonverbal in nature. Feelings of a very profound sort are involved. There is passion in sex and we have known and felt it in a wordless way. The attempt to use words throws us off. We feel awkward in our attempts to explain.

Avoiding the Pitfalls

So sometimes we lie. "The doctor brings the baby." We cheer ourselves up with the thought that it is a little lie. After all, the doctor *helps* bring the baby.

Or we postpone. "You'll understand better when you're older." There! That gets him off our back for now.

Or we get intellectual. We produce elaborate charts

and drawings to explain reproduction. This is far beyond him, but if the experts say it's important to tell a child about sex, why tell we will! This could be called a compliance dodge. We tell the facts, but in such a way that he can't understand them.

Or we hope he will understand about sex differences by seeing us undressed. But nudity doesn't really present the facts. An unseen vagina is a fact, but a child wouldn't know about it by looking. What nudity *does* do is generally stop communication. Children who have seen a lot usually do not ask questions. They are too mixed up to know where to begin. Adult exposure can wither discussion as effectively as charts and graphs. It is another way of saying, "Look, but don't ask." Further, it presents the child with a real dilemma, for he has no way to discharge his own body tensions.

Or we get poetic. "It's beautiful when people love." The child presses for more information than mother would like to give. But she's been told to be truthful so she takes the plunge. "It's like kissing," she says bravely. "The Daddy puts the penis in the Mommy's vagina when they want to have a baby."

"I think that's disgusting," says four-year-old Peggy. Her idea of the genitals is connected to bathroom activity.

"You must have done it three times," says Ted, counting on his kindergarten fingers.

"Wait till I tell Craig," yells Tommy. "He thinks you get babies at the hospital."

No wonder parents hope schools will do the job. Or the clergy. Or anybody else.

Straight Talk Is Best

Is there any way we can go about educating children in a practical fashion that avoids these pitfalls? If stretching the truth, postponing, sidestepping, demonstrating, and intellectualizing don't teach, what will?

Talking will but it is talking of a special kind. It is not just giving the facts in the form of a lecture. The talk that is most effective comes in response to questions that the child himself asks, and parents are often surprised at how early these questions come. That is because your child is enormously interested in himself and is trying to understand himself in relation to everything he sees and hears. When you respond to him in terms of issues that concern him, you are able to be more on target. Then you can concentrate on answering simply and to the point. As you hear him out further, you can help him with his perceptions, which are quite likely to be askew. Clarification will follow naturally if you know what he is thinking.

At nursery school, playground, or swimming pool your child will undoubtedly see other children un-clothed. While I espouse as much modesty as you can muster at home, I am not sure you will find a lot of support for this in public places. Somewhere, whether at nursery school or elsewhere, he will have seen another child being toileted, and you will find him struggling with his first major sexual issue—the issue of sexual diff-erence. This is what concerns the child at about age two, and this is what requires explanation.

Very understandably, he assumes that everyone is made like himself. It is quite a shock to discover others are made differently. So, somewhere between age two and three, you must slowly help him to recognize that everyone is made as he or she is supposed to be. The children he sees are intact, and so is he. His understand-ing of this is important in building self-acceptance. His self-esteem may then proceed normally. It may take quite a while before he fully accepts this recognition of difference. His limited ability to comprehend what he sees often conflicts with stories he concocts to explain what is not a very simple matter to his small brain. Your main task at this early time is to ask what he thinks. Try not to laugh at his speculations. Then set him straight.

Arthur, two, put small toy trucks in his swimming trunks at the YMCA swimming classes he attended with his mother. He kept shouting "Boke!" Then he ran home, stripped his clothes off, refused to put them back on, and strutted around with a belligerent air.

This strange behavior continued for some time. Then his mother suddenly realized "boke" meant "broke" and his concerns were for the ladies he saw undressed who were not endowed as he was. The trucks in the swimsuit were to protect his vital member. The strutting said, "See, I'm intact. I'm really okay. Not 'boke' at all."

Once Arthur's mother realized that he was in the normal "who's got what" stage, his strange behavior became understandable. She could then reassure him. She even went further and dressed him for swimming at home, bypassing the locker room, so as not to encounter the adult nudity the swimming pool fostered.

Clearing Up Confusion

In this phase you tell them boys have a penis. Girls have a vagina. It is a tube that is inside. You can't see it but it is there. All people were born the way they were supposed to be. Half the people in the world are girls and women; half are men and boys. No one changes from one to the other. Both sexes are important and parts are made as they are supposed to be. Try to do this slowly, over a period of time. Let your explanations come in response to questions.

You try not to laugh as their wish for magic overrides their good sense. They go back to early notions even after you've clarified the realities. This is a rumination that helps them digest their new knowledge. You may wonder why I stress the importance of clarifying mixups when children often persist in repeating misinformation even after you've explained things. It is because the process of being set straight, though requiring repetition, takes much of the fear and tension out of normal mental mixups at the time when distortions are most likely to occur. It's a bit like digging up new soil for a growing garden but recognizing that you have to weed as you go.

The next step is additional enlightenment. This means talking as you have already done but with an extra tuning into what your child is telling you. It is a dialogue that recognizes that the child has grown in his ability to understand. This is possible somewhere between the ages of three and five. (It can start earlier and go later, depending on the child's ability to verbalize and the questions he is struggling with.)

Early Questions

The child's first questions often relate to pregnancy. That is, after all, a highly visible process.

Here again, try to make your response part of a genuine dialogue if you can. Ask him what he's heard or what he thinks of the big tummy he sees. This enables two helpful things to happen:

1. It gives you time to collect your wits and to figure out what you think!

2. It enables you to educate in a way that is more to the point.

All he really needs to hear at this time is that the baby grows in a special place near Mommy's tummy but not in it. You can give it a name—womb or uterus—if he asks for it. Sometimes he mixes it up and talks about the lady swallowing something. You correct him. "No, it's not *in* the tummy. It's *near* the tummy."

You may find that he persists in his confusion as you hear him repeat his error six months or a year later. This is because the young child's view of the entrances and exits of the body is fairly primitive. Just tell him again. The simplest explanation is the best, especially when it's in response to a question he has.

The next question may be, "Where did I come from?"

Answer: "You grew inside of Mommy."

He may notice pregnant women or animals. You can talk about everybody in the world having a mommy. You explain that dog mommies make puppies and cat mommies make kittens. Each animal makes a baby like itself.

"But how did I start? How did I get in there?"

You can tell him about a tiny egg that the mommy's body makes. You can relate the process to other living things. When he wants to know how the baby grows inside, tell him about the cozy place the baby rests in. He is fed by a cord that gives the baby food until he or she is ready to come out. It takes nine months before a baby is ready. The baby needs that time to grow from a tiny egg into a real person.

Later Questions

This may be all that is necessary for some time. Later new questions may come.

"Where does the baby come out?"

You counter with your question, "What do you think?"

"I think the daddy cuts the mommy open with a knife," said Jennifer.

"No", said Robby. "The doctor does it."

"No," you answer. "When the baby is ready to come out, it starts pushing. It pushes out of the place it's been growing, into a tube called the vagina. That's the inside tube girls and ladies have. It pushes out of this tube head first. When it comes out, that is when we say a baby is born."

"But you said the vagina is near the wee-wee and BM place," worries Nancy, five. "How can a baby come out of such a tiny place?"

"It stretches," you reply, "like a rubber band."

"Did that happen to me?" she asks.

"Yes, and to everybody else."

"Well, maybe to everybody else," says five-year-old Allen, "but not to me." Denial of what they hear is very common. Don't worry about it. It's part of the yes-no process of absorption.

The next question may concern what part the father plays. This is generally the most difficult topic to discuss. But at some point—perhaps when the child is four or five (perhaps somewhat later)—he will want to know.

"I know about you," said Beth to her mother. "You borned me. But what about Daddy? Why is he my daddy? How did he get to be a daddy anyhow?"

This questioning may be more direct than what most of us hear. But in some form or other the question *does* come.

Beth's mother seized her opportunity.

"It takes two people to make a baby. A daddy and a mommy. The daddy's body makes something called sperm; the mommy's body makes the egg. When the egg and the sperm meet, that is the beginning of a baby."

The Big Question

That is often sufficient for some time. You don't want to overwhelm a child with information before he requests it. When he finally asks how the sperm you've told him about meets the egg you've told him about, you are faced with The Question. By this time, you've done a good part of the educating. This preliminary talking makes the description of intercourse not as difficult a task as you had thought.

You can tell your child that when a mommy and daddy love each other they want to hug each other. They sleep together and when they love, the sperm comes out of the daddy's penis and enters the mommy's vagina, where it meets the egg that the mommy's body has made. This is called fertilizing. When an egg is fertilized, it is the beginning of a baby.

Your child might not react at all to this information. Yet it is still worthwhile to have answered him. Honesty builds a relationship that provides a channel for future communication. It tells him that when he talks to you, you don't turn him off.

Other Aids

If he wants more information than you can offer, don't hesitate to use a book. This is also helpful for the nonverbal child who doesn't ask questions at all. In the latter case, leave the book around when he shows interest, or leave it around to elicit interest. That is better than plunging in when he hasn't asked. You can read the book to him. I particularly like *The Wonderful Story of How You Were Born** by Sidonie Matsner Gruenberg because it is simply written and acknowledges the feeling side as well as the factual side of conception.

If necessary, you can draw pictures. (You may need a book yourself to remember how the Fallopian tubes look.) This goes along with the modesty I've recommended. Children aren't allowed to see you nude because that neither clarifies their thinking nor neutralizes their excitement. Talk and more talk, books, and pictures do the job better because they explain things calmly and accurately.

If your child catches you at an inappropriate time for explanations—such as when you're on your way to a wedding and his piping voice asks, "When is the baby coming?" or when your very proper aunt is visiting and he asks you when he is going to make sperm like Daddy —stop him. Tell him these are private matters and not to be talked about with other people. Tell him you will explain what he wants to know later. But be sure to get back to him. Here again, your reliability is underscored.

*(New York: Doubleday, 1970).

Children are generally tactful about this when you educate them as to what is socially appropriate and what is not.

The Privacy Debate

Modesty is not easy to achieve in an era where swimming pools, restaurants, school lockers, and campsites fail to provide for privacy in dressing and toileting. Public facilities often separate the sexes, but they do not separate adults from children. You might find yourself explaining to a little girl that she will grow up one day to look like that lady getting into her bathing suit, but it is a difficult concept for her to grasp. She doesn't yet have the thinking ability to process what she is staring at, and she can't relate that body to her own. A boy has a similar problem because his size sense is distorted. One four-year-old, watching a man urinate, said, "His pee-pee is making a waterfall!" Since one cannot police the world, all I would recommend here is that you do your best (when you can) to arrange for privacy and allow talk about what they see when you can't.

Nursery school teachers sometimes toilet young children together in the belief that this will help the children accept sexual differences without being troubled by the size discrepancy. There are arguments to be made on both sides of the question. Even at home, parents may feel that young children can be bathed or toileted together, that it is a natural way for the toddler to learn about differences, particularly when the parent is ready to respond to the questions that are bound to come up. I would object to this if you see the children becoming too stimulated by mutual looking and if they get out of hand with silliness and fighting—two very disguised ways of showing body excitement. You may see something of this nature when you find you take a calm child swimming and a certified lunatic jumps into the water. This is a time for looking into what he has observed and

176

for recognizing he may be showing you anxiety about his observations. Here your knowledge of child development is a truly genuine asset. It enables you to clarify what is upsetting him and to set him straight. After all, his anxiety rests on mighty false premises.

There are mixed messages in our culture about sex and privacy that can easily confound parents as to the best way to go. Openness in terms of sexual activity and language has been equated with mental health by some. In this view the insistence on privacy is thought to lead to inhibition. This current pendulum swing away from an earlier more prudish time has brought its own spate of troubles, however. Many of our children are so busy being uninhibited they have a problem in focusing on school work. Or in meeting realistic expectations. Some of the children sent to me for hyperactivity by neurologists who have eliminated the physical basis for this behavior have proved to be overstimulated children who don't know what to do with the openness around them.

Sometimes an analogy is drawn to primitive tribes where one may admire the freedom, lack of restraint, and fewer sexual hang-ups suffered by the adults in these cultures. This is a false comparison because children in our society are growing up in a very different world, one that requires self-control and that values privacy. Unwittingly, I think, we are overloading our children's circuits by the amount of openness we are permitting them to see. Even parents who have not agreed with me philosophically have found the level of excitement in their homes reduced dramatically when they have become more modest. What makes any of this hard to prove is that some children are managing fine despite nudity in the home. So you will be deciding for yourselves about whether to change your privacy requirements or not. Certainly if you do, do it gradually. You may be surprised when your young child demonstrates his pleasure in the change by insisting on privacy for himself. You may find this concept useful even with siblings of the same sex.

One last word on sex education: eventually, when your children are grown, they may accuse you of never having told them the facts. It's a strange business, this forgetting. But you will have helped them despite their faulty memory because in the part of the childish mind where demons once played, you introduced reason and clarity.

15.
Divorce

"Who do I belong to?" asked Tommy, four, after he was told his parents were getting divorced. His first concern was for himself. His clear statement of anxiety testifies to the preschooler's understanding that he can't make it on his own and that someone has to take responsibility for him.

The Loyalty Conflict

For the young child, divorce marks a change that affects his life in a very unique way. His affections—or disaffections, as the case may be—are split and he is not, as in the case of death, part of a group that is left to mourn together. The comfort of unity in grief is denied him. It can make for great feelings of loneliness. As he feels affection for one parent, a loyalty conflict ensues about the other. Of course, if one parent has been openly brutal, this conflict is lessened, since presumably the more appropriate parent takes command and in effect rescues him. Even then the child may feel an attachment, unrealistic though it may seem to the observer. Most divorces, however, are not so clear-cut.

Marriages may flounder on adult incompatibilities of a subtler sort, and these may be unknown to the young child.

He loves both his parents, and he does not see them realistically with lives and interests of their own. The divorce comes as a blow to him, despite the fact that he may have witnessed violent arguments and been worried by outbursts of anger and periods of separation. After all, he is the result of this parental union, and he is tied to the issue of divorce in the same way he was tied to the marriage. His parents may get a divorce, but he cannot. He continues to belong to them even if they no longer belong to each other.

In this age of divorce some of my language may seem antiquated. Do we "belong to each other" anymore? Is there not now more of a stress on individual fulfillment? Are there not mothers who do not wish to marry? I cannot argue these issues because each family has its own unique way of coping with the current explosion in the divorce rate. What is happening to the American family in general is the subject of much study and speculation today and final conclusions (if indeed there will ever be any) are not in yet. There are reports that show divorce is good for children, since they suffer when there is conflict in the home. Staying together has proved a barren journey for many who tried. There are other reports that show divorce has aftereffects, not always envisaged by those who hoped it would solve problems. No doubt some couples are happier for having divorced, and some are not. The important point is that divorce is more common now than it ever was, and the need to help children cope with it is, therefore, greater than ever before.

Adult Responsibility

It may not be possible for the principals of the divorce to think clearly about their children's needs in the face of rancor and bitterness. Everything that happened earlier in the marriage exerts an influence. Past divisiveness will have an effect on money and custody arrangements. What is best for children has more often been a matter of the viewed best interests of each parent as dealt with by his or her attorney, rather than the needs of the child. Some couples attempt counseling first, and this is certainly worth a try. Sometimes compromises are reached that restore a balance for a while. Even if the union is ultimately broken, talking ahead of time gives parents a chance to figure out the best way to talk to their children about the divorce. Much will depend on whatever good feelings remain.

What one hopes for is the ability on the part of parents to keep focused on their children's needs despite their very strong differences. The idea might be to make a success of the divorce for the sake of the children even though the marriage itself was unsuccessful. It can be a double burden for the partners involved; for while they are struggling to settle their own lives (amid feelings of anger, hurt, revenge, resignation, or whatever), they are still having to deal with the future as well as the feelings of their children.

The temptation to use the child as a weapon in the battle is great on the part of both antagonists. It takes some effort to resist this very human impulse.

"What Will Happen to Me?"

The main issue for the child is how this new arrangement will affect his life. Until he is older he does not consider how it affects yours.

So you tell him, "We are separating and are not going to live together. No, it's not your fault. Mommy and Daddy don't get along and think it better if we live apart."

His fear that he will be abandoned because he doesn't get along with the absent parent may or may not be voiced. Talk about this anyhow.

"Daddy is still your Daddy and he loves you. He is going to come visit on Tuesday and Sunday."

This type of explanation will suffice. Children do not need to know all the details that led to the divorce. Their primary concern is what will happen to them, not what happened between you.

Anger toward either or both parents may be expressed. Try to allow it. When loyalty conflicts surface, they do less damage. You know what he is coping with and are then in a position to help him clarify his feelings.

"I can see you are mad at me. That's okay. It's a hard time for you."

He may see you in tears or overhear you in an angry outburst. You can acknowledge what your feelings are, but still you must reassure him.

"We are still your Mommy and Daddy even if we don't live together anymore."

He needs to know that his needs will be met.

"You will live with me. Daddy will visit. Both of us care for you."

"But I want to live together!" he storms. You acknowledge his wish but tell him it can't be. Honesty helps him over the long haul.

Often children are the most difficult to handle just when the parent or parents desperately need peace and quiet. The child is likely to blame the parent he is left with, since that's the one who is handy. In most cases this is the mother. She finds herself trying to maintain a home at the same time that her child accuses her of destroying his.

Mothers who are left to raise children by themselves feel the inequity of divorce. They are the rearers and the daily discipliners and therefore the ones who get the brunt of their children's mixed feelings.

"It's your fault!" a child may say openly. "If you'd been nice to Daddy, this wouldn't have happened!"

A child sometimes glorifies an absent parent. The parent who is away in turn may encourage this by becoming a "treat" person for the few hours spent with the child. This is a disservice to the child; it is self-serving rather than helpful. Counseling (with the aim of helping the child cope with a problem of considerable magnitude in his life) may prove useful to either or both parents when the divorce is definite. Talking it over with a counselor who understands what a divorce means to a child can help the parent who bears the major caretaking job.

One parent cannot be both mother and father to the child, despite the wish to make up for his loss. Talking about the situation with your child puts it in a context. There are still a mother and a father, even though the living situation is different. Even if the other parent is absent permanently, allow the child to talk about it, and tell him the facts so that he doesn't feel someone important to him has dropped into a void. This helps mitigate his feeling of loss. Even though the message is painful for him, don't sidestep it. Don't make the mistake of thinking, "Out of sight, out of mind." He is churning things over, and you keep in touch when you communicate. Talking about loss doesn't restore the past, but neither does it bury it in an unrealistic way. Talk helps the child to master a trauma. Despite the pain of divorce, children can cope when given facts and help with their feelings.

Their greatest need is to have the main facts outlined for them in a clear fashion. Specifics are the best. Where you will live. Where Daddy will live. (Seeing the place where the departing parent will be living helps root him in the child's mind.) Since the child under-five worries so much about separation, making the links of time and place for him is important. If the absent parent moves far away, pictures of the new place should be sent. Letters and phone calls help.

If the future is uncertain and these matters are unclear for a time, reassure the child with, "We don't know yet," but then you add, "As soon as we know, we will tell you." This, too, is a bridge to answers that will be coming later.

Outside Help

Groups that encourage the sharing of common experiences may prove useful. One of these, Parents Without Partners, has chapters in most cities. Their national headquarters is located at 7910 Woodmont Avenue, Bethesda, Maryland 20814 (301-654-8850). The Child Study Association of America, 50 Madison Avenue, New York, New York 10010, has pamphlets on the subject of divorce and a guide as to where and when these groups meet. If there isn't a group in your city, you can form one with others facing similar problems. Group support can be particularly helpful at times of shared trauma. Activity in your own behalf can relieve your feeling of helplessness. Acting on the reality of the separation and coping with the real changes it makes in your life help your child more than behavior that supports the notion that you can be all things to him. The wish on your part to repair the damage is real. It can be done best by acknowledging the break and dealing with the feelings that attend it.

It is not easy to help your child when you yourself are coping with such a difficult experience. Divorce may bring feelings of humiliation and diminished self-worth. The task of helping your child in the midst of these feelings can seem overwhelming, and it is important for you to have some support and relief at this time. Don't feel you have to stay home all the time to compensate for your spouse's absence. But do recognize that your leaving your child has special significance now. You have become doubly important to him because he may still think magically. "If Daddy can leave, maybe she will, too." So now you may see more clinging, more upset when you go. This will subside in time as you allow your child time for the feelings of sadness and anger to be voiced. Your reassurance that you will always be back is very meaningful to him.

Because you as custodial parent may be most depleted just as your child is most needy, you may find you have trouble being the tower of strength you want to be for him. Here a good friend can be of help. She or he can talk to your child and can once more provide the facts he needs to hear. He learns slowly that all is not lost. Friends and family can help reassure him that everybody in his world isn't disappearing. Active support on the part of these people—treats given, excursions taken— also break into the gloom of the experience for your child, enabling him to be relieved of his suffering inter- mittently. The continuity of nursery school or play group is helpful as he sees his little world go on. It provides some routine organization for him in the midst of the big change.

The key, of course, to the child's good adjustment is his relationship to you—the person who remains as care- giver. The dependability you offer helps him conquer his distrust and enables him to move on in his development. Counseling for you may be of real assistance at a time you find yourself shouldering these many responsibili- ties at once. Social agencies or private practitioners in social work, psychology, or child psychiatry may be use- ful here. Your family doctor or pediatrician is a good source for making the proper referral if you find that you need it.

Allow for a Period of Adjustment

The best possible arrangement would be to have every- thing else in the child's life remain the same in the midst of both the process of divorcing and the final legal break. Same house. Same school. Same friends. This is not al- ways possible because economic issues (and often money dissension) come rapidly to the fore in divorce. There are now to be two households instead of one. Nevertheless it is worthwhile trying to keep life as settled as possible for the kids for as long a time as possible. This gives them a chance to absorb the big turn their lives have taken. Then, if a move should be necessary, it need not feel as overwhelming. They will have more energy to devote to the new steps that will follow. As in other important matters in the lives of preschoolers, gradualism helps them to a more mature acceptance.

If you find you have to go to work, try to give your child some time to prepare for your absence. Otherwise he may feel as if he lost both parents simultaneously—one by divorce and the other by absence. See if you can arrange a divorce settlement that allows you to be home for a while before you leave your child with someone else. If this is not possible, do your best to find the right person to take care of your child. Have the housekeeper or sitter spend some time with you and your child before you leave (a week or a month, whatever you can arrange), and prepare to do a lot of listening to the feelings your child will verbalize about the changes in his life. Ideally, you should stay home for a few months—even a year—before returning to work. This may not be feasible financially, however, and much can be accomplished in a few weeks of explaining and contact with a new caretaker. Once again, the central point is getting your child to accept the realities of the situation. Again, it is your acknowledgement and verbalization of the child's feelings that help him to accept the facts.

Role of Non-Custodial Parent

In most cases it is the mother who retains custody of the children. If the father has custody, of course, the same recommendations hold.

The most important effort for the off-premises parent is making sure there is no abdication of the parental role (despite living elsewhere). The children need you more than ever. It will take time for them to absorb the fact that you are still the father (or the mother) even though they see you less. Young children relate to adults in terms of how they function for them, and I think when you can arrange to continue helping fulfill their needs (whether feeding, bathing, or playing together), it lets them know that you have remained a genuine participant in their lives.

Extra gifts are not necessary. The being together and being tuned in when you are together is more important. If civility exists between divorced parents, a helpful attitude between them can carry over into more casual visiting arrangements. If it is not so cordial a relationship, specific set times are useful. Here the child can plan ahead and look forward to visits that maintain the connection for him. The important issue is to keep one's promises about visits. If you must cancel, tell the children. Write letters and telephone when you must be away.

The reparative wish may be very great for the noncustodial parent. Try to sit on the very normal impulse to make up to them a lot. The casual things you used to do together are as good or better than elaborate outings. Watching a favorite TV program together is as good as going to a game. Ordinary activities shine in their own unique light because in an indirect way, they teach the child that daily life continues and that it very much includes you.

If you can, keep your business discussions about child support and other matters with the parent in residence separate from your visits with your child. In this way, not only are the children left out of what can be an acrimonious exchange, but they receive Father's full attention when they are with him.

When a father visits the children in his former wife's home, it can be helpful if she disappears. She can overlook small infractions of her standards as long as they are not excessive. If they are, the business discussions she has with her ex-spouse are a reasonable time to work these out. Times when the children are elsewhere are best. It may be an effort to refrain from pressing for details when the children return (what with feelings still running high for a time), but it is good if you can. This minimizes their loyalty conflict. It helps for them not to be put in the position of taking sides. The child appreciates the effort that is being made for him. You needn't pretend friendship if you don't feel any, but good manners and trying to be minimally civil helps everyone muddle through this difficult time better. If matters are pretty rock-bottom, you can talk to your child about your anger (he perceives it anyhow); then when you are polite, he will recognize your effort as good manners.

Defections

The approach is similar with a child who has been deserted by his mother.

"Mommy wasn't able to come for you," said a father in the face of his wife's running off. "She has a pretty bad problem. She wants to come and see you but her problem keeps her away." This is an attempt to soften the blow. While a reason is not an excuse—and the child may tell you so in no uncertain terms—telling him that his mother's defection is not directed against him can be of help until he is able to understand more. You can say, "It makes you angry and sad when Mommy doesn't come."

Smaller defections, such as when a parent says he will come but doesn't, can be just as difficult for the child to bear. Hopes are raised and shattered each time a promise is not kept. The other parent's unreliability, as a fact of the child's life, becomes painfully clear. It takes time for the child to recognize and accept this.

A father who has been awarded custody of his children and who, as family provider, will be away much of the time will need to find a housekeeper or caretaker to serve in lieu of mother. As with the working mother, careful selection is necessary.

All life is a risk. You may say, "Our marriage didn't work out. I'm sorry about that, but we had you and that is good." Working the sorrow out together can strengthen character, too. It should comfort you to know that while the parent who stays with the child gets most of the complaints, in the long run, the child knows who put in the effort.

Remarriage

The day comes when you remarry. Time has moved on and things have somehow fallen into place. You now feel you have found the right person, and you hope for a better life for you and your family. But it is important to remember that your children did not choose this new partner. It is you who chose him, and their loyalties may well be elsewhere. They may feel they are slighting their own family in taking the new person on so that you are placed in a no-win situation, just when life is looking up. If they don't like your mate, it's not pleasant, and if they do, they feel guilt about their other "own" parent.

All this means is that you have to help your new mate understand that the approach to the children has to be a slow one. He or she needs to recognize that the real parent is still the real parent and that he or she is a highly charged person and often an unsought figure for the children. Remarrieds find they face all sorts of rivalries and loyalty conflicts in the beginning of their new life. What can sustain both of you is the knowledge that slowly and over time ties generally develop, particularly if one is not trying too hard. Some wise person said that the important thing in a reconstituted family is to allow the children not to love you. Certainly fewer expectations can help you phase in gradually.

You are now a step-whatever, whose obligations and duties are not very clear except in fairy tales (where you have a very bad press). Adequate care-taking, a reasonable routine, and as much patience as you can muster will all help as you come into the situation as a friend. A relationship is an earned thing and it has to build in its own way. By taking your cues from the children, you will learn that it is *they* who finally determine what and who you are for them.

One new stepfather admitted a preference for being called by his first name rather than "Dad." At the same time, he took on expected fatherly functions—helping bathe the children, visiting nursery school, babysitting. The "easing in" approach didn't dictate feelings to anyone. These followed as the new family shared experiences together.

Discipline issues are often intensified in reconstituted families. Obligations and duties are frequently not clear and it requires some thinking ahead to set guidelines that include expectations (see Chapters Five, Six, and Seven on discipline) but that modify these to allow for verbalizing any distress and anger the child may be feeling. The "own" parent may do better with a parallel story about feelings, but he will be much more effective if he and the new mate stand together on what they expect from the children.

If you encourage the expression of feelings, don't be surprised to hear things you don't want to hear. (Try to remember that this expression of pent-up feelings ultimately allows them to give a better performance.) You can handle this by hearing them out and then by saying, "I'm glad you told me how you feel. Now, however, I expect you to behave and make an effort." The to and fro of facts and feelings goes on for a long time. Again, a united front, despite one's own often mixed feelings, helps children the most.

What ultimately gives you a place in the heart of the young child is your function in his life. As children are cared for by you—as they are fed, bathed, put to bed—

as they are reprimanded, told stories, bandaged, and hugged—they, too, respond to the effort you make. And as with all children, they know who is putting in the time.

The Reconstituted Family: A Study of Remarried Couples and Their Children by Lucille Duberman* is an excellent book that enlarges on these ideas in a useful way.

---

*(Chicago: Nelson-Hall Publishers, 1975)

16.
Trying to Solve the Dilemma

*A*s WE have seen from the foregoing chapters, mothers or the full-time caregivers who are doing the mothering of babies and toddlers are in a most basic sense human developers. They humanize the young, civilize them, transmit culture in the way they treat them. They are, in short, the child's first educators. Not in the reading and writing sense but in the sense of encouraging the steps that lead to emotional maturity. Because a child is so unfinished at birth, a mother has to steer for him for a long time, relinquishing to him very gradually those things he slowly learns to do for himself. This is education of a very high order. The love mother evokes in a child fuels his abilities and helps make him educable. In this mothering, whether from mother or a reliable substitute, the child profits by the strong feeling of security he receives. This is the basis of self-esteem. And it is what every mother wants for her children. How to use herself in the process of helping a child master developmental stages is a developmental step for the mother herself. The love tie is the vehicle that gets her over the normal rough spots of child rearing.

This is pretty fancy language for what mothers have always offered their children all over the world without even thinking about it. It requires restatement now because of the dilemma work outside the home presents for the mothers of this generation. I am struck, in my contact with working mothers, at how fragile and often lost this knowledge has become. It is important that mothers who are staying home with their children know that they are doing something valuable.

Restating the Importance of Mothering

Society once regarded the mothering function of women as not only basic to society but of great significance for the common good. This idea has been weakened considerably during the current push for women doing what is regarded as more important work. The satisfactions of mothering itself have been lost for many. That is why I have restated information about the vulnerability of the infant and the importance of his needs. It is knowledge we have to regain. When we do, it will influence the arrangements we make for our children, and this should benefit them accordingly. Trying to resolve the dilemma of whether to work or stay home requires, for women of today, close observation of how an infant grows.

When one observes how a baby and young child relate, one sees the importance of the caring relationship from the beginning. A nine-month-old has learned to love its mother and cares when she leaves. An eighteen-month-old who can manage an hour or two away from her may suddenly cling, cry, or develop a sleep disturbance. Their needs and feelings of safety are so intertwined with their special person, separation from that person feels like abandonment. Writer Graham Greene once said that to a young child, separation feels like being in the middle of a tunnel with no beginning or end. The child under-three finds that tunnel endless because he does not understand time. His mind hasn't formed the "go away, come back" concept. Awareness of this happens as he grows. The brief intervals when one leaves an infant in the first year provide an assimilable base for him to absorb this knowledge. His potential for loving grows in this holding environment. In this he is not unlike the premature infant (though much further along, of course) who requires time in a womblike environment to catch up. Human babies are not ready to go at birth. Their need for slow time with their parents is not a philosophical idea or a matter of style. Since a baby's feeling life begins in relation to them, the care they offer helps build an emotional structure that will serve for a lifetime. A house is not built from the roof down.

Individual Care

A working mother of two-and-a-half-year-old twins consulted me recently about her children's biting, hitting, and scratching in their day-care center. Their crying at night for hours before going to bed distressed her.

When I talked about children in the early years needing individual care rather than a group arrangement, she understood perfectly. This was not a disciplinary issue the children were exhibiting but a sign of distress. "In two years my husband's business will be stabilized and I'll be able to stay home," she told me. I do not know if the business could have waited if she had reversed her decision and had been home with the twins from the start. But she had never heard of the proper sequence— better to pay now, fly later. If she had, she and her husband might have planned differently.

When we consider how far a child comes in the early years, the importance of those years becomes clearer. From an "I'm for me first" mentality to consideration for others. From random messiness to orderliness and cleanliness. From no ability to tolerate frustration to some ability to take a turn, wait a little. The pleasure principle that dominates infant and toddler life yields only gradually to the reality principle—loosely defined as having to do what has to be done when it needs to be done—as in school, for example. This gradual mastery of the self does not just happen. A guiding hand helps make it happen, and the reason this guidance succeeds is that the person with the expectations is loved by the child. Pleasure in the relationship softens the hard issues of learning the "have to's" of life. When the storms of adolescence hit a decade later and the children pull away from family, there is a "core of us" inside them that helps them come back to the fold when the furor has subsided.

Being Home: Feelings of Isolation

This does not mean that there are not problems for the mother who stays home and mothers. There is the isolation that comes from often being the only mother on the block who is doing it. "I feel like I am mothering the whole community when the kids of mothers not home cluster at my house," said one mother to me recently. The loss such mothers feel today for a bygone security where pretty much everyone saw things the same way, where the expectations of women for mothering were part of the culture, is real. Such a mother has to search for other mothers who think as she does, to find people who feel that raising a family of happy, decent, ultimately useful people is a form of social action too. She has to struggle with balancing the protective part of parenting (not only electric outlets and household poisons, but ultimately the dangers of the street) with encouraging autonomy and independence. Often she finds that because of distance, she is more involved with her children's social life than she wants to be. The at-home mother may feel she is half-woman, half-station wagon as she chauffeurs children who are no longer allowed the wholesome venturing out of an earlier time. The lack of recognition in the culture for what she is doing can hurt self-esteem, even if she is certain of her choice and is satisfied with it.

Being at Work: the Emotional Conflict

For the mother who goes back to work after her baby's birth, the emotional pull of love for her new baby makes leaving him unexpectedly painful. There seems to be a biological bedrock here. Women are nurturers as well as givers of life, and this has nothing to do with economic conditions or career choices.

No matter which way a woman decides to raise her children (whether to be at home or to employ a substitute for herself as she works), she struggles with feelings coming from the road not taken. The woman who goes back to work when her infant is young knows, when another raises her child, that she will have to share the role. She is invested emotionally in him but much of his time is spent with someone else. This is the source of her concern, and yes, of her guilt. She may feel she is being separated from her child for too long a time. She may recognize that even a good day-care center is not the answer, that it does not provide the constancy of care she wants for her baby.

Admitting this to herself is even more stressful to her. Some mothers, in an effort to make up for this, keep their children up late so they can be with them longer. The trade-off here is that the children are frequently tired and irritable in the morning and less able to adapt to their caregivers. Other mothers may breastfeed long after a reasonable time for weaning has passed. This is an effort to keep children close, to make up for the all-day separation. Mothers do not want to be lesser people in their children's lives and try in this way to offer physical closeness in an effort to redress a loss.

Choices for the Working Mother

How to resolve the dilemma?

It is not easily done.

It requires, for those of you who work, keeping a close eye on what is best for your child, given that you are away from him at a critical time in his life. The first step may be the hardest—admitting to yourself that this separation from you is a stress for your child. (You have already learned that it is one for you.) If you can look this basic premise in the face, so to speak, the avenues for working toward a better plan for your child's care will come clearer.

There are three major issues for you to consider:

1. the time when you leave your child to begin work;
2. the length of time spent away from your child as you work;
3. the quality of substitute care you find for him.

Within these major planning issues lie a series of choices. Understanding alternatives regarding each one of these can help you clarify your thinking.

The first issue of when to go to work reflects the thrust of this book. Staying home with your child for the first three years of his life is best. It is the best minimum to help him establish himself. He is formed sufficiently by then to be able to adapt to a good day-care program that is child-centered and well-run. (This does not mean that staying home with children through all the years of childhood is a lesser choice. Children, even older ones, benefit from mother, or caregiver, being there when they come home from school. Sharing all of childhood with your youngster, however, is, again, an individual decision.) Next best for the working mother who can arrange it is staying home for two years. Here again, the issue of more time versus less with your child is the major consideration. But even one year at home with baby is not a small contribution.

A caregiver who took care of children in her own home told me, "When I get a one-year-old, there is already a little person in there. He is more together." She added thoughtfully, "I have more to work with."

The second issue of how long a day to be away from your child is hard to examine because it is largely dictated by the work place. In this area women need to work together for change, because business and industry may learn, if the value of individual care for children is recognized, that adaptation to part-time work need not mean loss of productivity in the long run. Many leaders, fathers themselves, could benefit from learning more about children's needs. Each family needs to consider for itself how this may be done, even in today's not-hospitable-to-mothers climate.

But even given the current situation—can you cut down on time spent at work? A shorter week? A shorter day? Flextime? If you are in school, perhaps fewer courses taken during this period? Maybe a shared plan of responsibility for care with father or friend? Here again, you are working to give yourself and your baby as much time together as you can. When working mothers who have consulted me have taken steps such as these, they have been delighted with the benefits they see for themselves and their children. They see more of an attachment to and a greater depth of relationship with their children. Substitute caretakers of very young children with whom I have spoken have commented spontaneously about the benefits of mothers working fewer hours (and therefore requiring less babysitting for their children). What is nice about even some adjustment to give more time at home is that it allows your child the pleasure of your company and reduces the amount of anxiety he feels because of separation from you.

Finally, the quality of the substitute you secure for

yourself is important. Individual care by a loving mature person is of prime importance. Here your child makes a relationship with a dear person who is there for him. This aids his emotional growth. For those lucky enough to have extended family nearby who can and want to help, the choices are much easier.

Considering that there are many older people who have retired and may wish to work part-time, it may be possible to find a lady who has had experience raising her own children, who can use some extra money to add to her social security check, and who perhaps enjoys being needed (at a time when society judges she may not be). A college student may serve as a good part-time babysitter, but may not prove best in the long run because one would like a promise of long-term commitment. Try to have someone sign on for three years at a minimum.

Phasing in Your Substitute

If possible, it helps if you can be home for two weeks or more during the phasing in of the new person. This allows your child to get to know her and to absorb her presence gradually. The caretaker is educated in this interval (even if everyone is uncomfortable at first) to the family's ways. This time together gives you a chance to build your own relationship with this woman. Trust takes time and as you see how she manages, you gain confidence in her ability to take on your most important possession. Then you leave the child gradually. An hour the first day, two hours the second, three hours the third. This is not a waste of time and money. Your child is absorbing the new person; you are feeling less uneasy; your work life can only gain from this peace of mind. If you cannot take time to phase a new person in, have someone your child knows who can take the time to do it. It's a way of easing the transition.

Talk to your child during this time about what is happening. (You never know, even with young babies, when they begin to understand.) Introduce the new lady by having her visit. Your staying with her at first phases her into his life in your safe presence. When you must go, say when you will be leaving, say when you will be back. Show him by the gradualness of the good-byes that the "go away-come back" phenomenon really holds. With children, small slow changes are better integrated than large, all-at-once ones.

As you finally separate for the work day, you can make some symbolic gestures that help him keep you in his mind. Call from work. (He may not talk but he will listen.) Let your child see your work place. Leave your picture with him, or maybe a tape of you explaining things. Perhaps an article of clothing. For the very young child, this can be tangible evidence that you will come back.

Expect crash time when you come home because transitional times are the hardest for children. Sometimes they are happy to see you. Often they are angry you've been gone. What I hope you can do is allow time to hear them out. Sometimes making more time in the morning to hear sad or angry feelings allows them to cope better during the day. Remember that distress is a sign of attachment so in a real sense, *bad* is good. (If you don't see distress, it doesn't mean they are *not* attached. All I mean is that listening will give you clues as to what is going on.) Then you can explain, tell them what's coming next. They hear better when their feelings have aired. As with all interaction with young children, you are dealing with both fact ("I must leave"), feeling ("It's hard for you"), and comfort ("I will call during lunch"). This recognition of where they are coming from helps support the attachment bond you are working hard to maintain.

Trust of the caretaker develops slowly over time. The best situation is one where you talk with your substitute together at frequent intervals so that you learn to understand each other. It may be necessary to structure a time in the work week to ensure this, perhaps on the phone. You want to know what is going on in the day—how she is helping your child manage a stage, what has upset him, what is going well. You will be watching to see whether she is tuning into him, learning his cues, doing, in short, the things you would be doing if you were there. This is an extra burden you carry. In addition to Father who, as a parent, also needs to be given information about his child, you now need time to include a third person in your daily menage with all the to-ing and fro-ing of personal interchange such a relationship requires.

This tie to the caretaker is perhaps the most significant part of the arrangements you have made for your child's care. It keeps you in the picture even though you are away. You are filled in and can fill her in. Your child can be treated in like fashion by you and your helper so that he is not confused by differing standards, different styles. Obviously it is never a perfect fit, but the effort to make it work with some consistency is well worth the time. It is your child who benefits from the extra effort.

Your child will love this person if all goes well. Little ones often call both you and the caretaker "Mommy." It can hurt you to see love go to an outsider, but consider it a plus. Love takes practice and the ability to love comes from love given, attachment formed. This is why you have worked so hard to find the right person.

Separation from the Caretaker

Despite promises and good intentions, a caretaker leaves. A husband gets transferred; other claims dominate the caretaker's plans. She may feel close to your family, but she has a life apart.

Try to make her separating from your child a gradual one. Just as you put in some hard work in the phasing-in period, you are now putting some thought into the phasing-out period. It may be hard to remember, if you are disappointed in this woman, that she is somebody special to your youngster. Here again you are considering what is best for your child, putting aside your own disappointment and anger. Keep a picture of the lady. Have her call your child. If she remains in town, visit. Here again, you are firming up your child's ability to clarify who is who for him, what is happening to him. He won't feel responsible for the change (magical thinking operates here also) as he hears the facts from you. You may need to talk about good-bye feelings. You may see your child be sad, angry, or fearful about the change. That is normal too. Sadness, anger, and fear are the feelings evoked by the loss of a loved person.

On the positive side, remember that all is not lost when this person leaves. You and your husband provide continuity for your child. And the more you have been involved in keeping his interests in mind, the better he will adjust to the changes that are taking place.

Other Child-Care Alternatives

If you can't arrange for an individual caretaker for your child, family day care (another mother home with her children taking yours in) might be an alternative to consider. Here again, interviewing is important, references are important, *and* some assessment of how she is as a mother with *her* children needs to be made. You need to see if this is a person on your wavelength. States vary in this connection but it is important to check licensure, number of children in the home, and other guidelines. The fewer the children, the better. If her older children go to school, she will have more time for your child. No more than two children under two years of age is best, or the individual attention you want cannot be given. Even a good caretaker can't give more than custodial care if there are too many children in the home.

The issue of day-care centers for the under-three takes me too far afield from my premise that individual care for up-to-three's is best. After that age, I think they can be a helpful alternative if the staff is good, the ratio of children to teacher is small, and they address the issues of feeling and separation instead of having children deny them. Visiting and observing will give you some idea of the quality of care.

Social Action for Child Care

The United States is the only industrialized country without laws providing leave for a mother of a newborn. Seventy-five other countries provide not only leaves but guarantees of jobs when mothers return. Sweden, for example, provides for a year's leave with a job guaranteed upon return. There is some payment to the mother during that year. In France, there is a two-year leave; Hungary allows three years off with a job guarantee. Spain not only allows for a three-year maternity leave, but adds another provision that permits a parent to work half time after that until a child is six*. These arrangements recognize the importance of mothering to the young.

We need a push from mothers to support leave for mothers of newborns without loss of employment. Currently, there is pressure for a law that allows a mother to be home with her child for four months after delivering. While this is certainly an effort in the right direction, children need more than what mothers can give in a four-month interval before returning to work. Further efforts need to be expended on strengthening family life on many levels, and on pressing for fathers to be involved financially after divorce. The media has given wide coverage to social ills that affect family life—child abuse, threats of molestation, etc. But the needs of the young for mothering, for the emotional base on which to develop, have been largely ignored. Industry and gov-

---

*William and Wendy Dreskin, *The Day Care Decision* (New York: M.E. Evans and Company, 1983), 143–44.

ernment act as though it's not their business. It should be. Special interests lobby for their preferences. It is time we lobbied for ours. The future of our children deserves no less.

Need for Community Action

Yet, a recognition of the need for support for the mother at home should not be lost in the face of the larger social action that is needed. The extended family of the past that not only enriched a young child's life but whose members served as babysitters and as people on call for emergencies is but a heard-about story to many young families today. The emotional drain of rearing the young (never easy at any time) becomes even harder when there is not a grandmother near, a favored aunt to consult, someone to step in to help during a crisis. Just at the time when young parents are trying to live up to their ideals of maturity and attempting to be the nurturers of their children, the landscape for them is lunar, devoid of other adults who could absorb some of the daily fallout of ordinary child rearing.

This can put families where Mother *is* at home full-time also at risk. Love and the satisfactions of parenting are real, but the emotional capacities of adults vary. There are ambivalent feelings in all of us at times. We love our children yet sometimes we can barely stand them. We want the genuine love feelings we have for our young to be sustained in the face of the ordinary hassles children put us through. The loss of community today for those doing the important work of raising children makes the job harder.

Some community agencies are beginning to address the issue. Churches are offering babysitting services in "Mother's Day Out" programs. Libraries are expanding their educational role to include special programming for mothers and children. The YMCA in my city, Cleveland, offers a course entitled "BYOB (Bring Your Own

Baby)," where mothers meet and share experiences. The Jewish Community Center in Cleveland began Family Place in 1982 and saw an idea whose time had come take off. Here a large room was given to parents who could drop in with their young children at any time. There are toys for the children, books for the parents to read, and a small professional staff available to discuss child-rearing issues when asked. Nonsectarian and welcoming, Family Place has been particularly helpful to newcomers to town. Mothers themselves have started baby-sitting co-ops, meeting other women and ensuring that their children are supervised by reasonable people when they leave. These co-ops have enabled them to take courses or participate in community activities of interest to them. Altruism on the part of parents and love for children is not enough. Mothers' needs for adult companionship, some intellectual and physical outlets, and just plain time for themselves is also real. Being respected as a person with interests of her own makes a woman a better mother. Feeling good about oneself enables one to cope better with a child's needs and demands.

For the mother at home, what I am suggesting is knitting a community where none exists. One woman physician I know, who has put her career on hold, told me she is going to start a Family Place when she moves to another city. "All you need is a room in a church or a center and a coffee urn," she said. "The rest will come." If networking is the buzzword today for working together to achieve a goal, it is also a serviceable one for the mother at home.

The benefit to all of us in thinking in terms of the needs of children is substantial—both for them and for us. Child rearing is a stewardship that infers obligation. Putting our young in the center of our thinking acknowledges this and commits us to do our best for them despite other claims. Each one of you will find your own way through the dilemma facing women today. Redressing the balance of adult options with understanding about what children require enables you to make more knowledgeable decisions. Supporting your child's right to matter in these uneasy times is quite a legacy to leave behind.

for explaining negative
emotions, 102–3
for middle child, 101–2
and new baby, 100–101
sibling rivalry explored
through, 99–100
use of, 44, 96–99
Parents
as partners, 141–42
as united front, 143–44, 152
Parents Without Partners,
142, 184
Play
father's role in, 145–46
four- to five-year-olds',
73–75
functions of, 158–59
importance of, 80–81
three- to four-year-olds', 71
toddlers', 69
Potty chair, 28–29
Pregnancy, child's questions
about, 172
Presents, 141
Privacy. *See also* Modesty
child's need for, 94
in home
functions of, 163–64
gradual introduction of,
160–61
need for, 155–56
and sex education, 176–78
Punishment, 65–66

Q

Quality time, 8–9
Quantity time, 8–9

R

Rectal thermometer, 46
Regression
after developmental
advances, 36–37

after hospitalization, 135
in response to grief, 124
Remarriage, 189–91
Responsibility
child's sense of, 61
and school work, 82–83
teaching, 82
necessity for, 58–60
Rest time, 71
Roughhousing, 80

S

Safety
and discipline, 74
with toddler, 17, 62–63
Self-control
teaching, 63–65
in third year, 26
Self-esteem
child's, after toilet
training, 36
child's development of,
192
Selfishness, 87–88
Self-mastery, 151–52, 195
and toilet training, 36,
151–52
Separation
children's reaction to, 106,
193–94
child's behavior at,
meaning of, 4–5
early, length of, 107–8
emotional response to,
109–11, 113–14
dealing with, 114–15
infant's feelings about,
13–14
mastery of, 111–12
in second year, 19–20
sudden, 115–16
Sex education, 150–67
and bed problems, 164–65
benefits of modesty in,
159–60
books as aids in, 175

in second year,
  development of, 16–19
Toilet training
  accidents in, 32–33
  clean-up after, 34–36, 39
  age for, 22, 23
  beginning timetable for,
    29–31
  and character
    development, 27
  child's role in, 38–39
  as educational process, 27,
    39, 46–47
  emotions in, 43–45
  enemas in, 45–46
  equipment, 28–29
  later steps in, 40–43
  messiness in, 32–33, 42
  at nap time, 41
  at night, 41, 42
  preparation for, 28
  preparatory stage, 39
  readiness for, signs of, 22,
    28
  role changes in, 26–27
  and self-mastery, 36, 151–52
  and sex education, 165, 176
  steps, 31–32, 39
  timetable for, 38
  use of praise in, 34
Training pants, 29, 39
Tricycle syndrome, 36
Two-year-old. *See also*
  Terrible twos; Toddler

discipline issues with,
  69–71
thinking processes of, 17,
  19, 52

U

Understanding fallacy, 53–54
Unlimited love, myth of,
  50–51

V

Vacation
  child-free, 108–9
  preparing child for
    separation of, 109–11
Verbal abuse, 89–90
Verbalization. *See* Talking

W

Whining, 88–89
Willpower, development of,
  46
Working mother. *See*
  Mother, working

ABOUT THE MAKING OF THIS BOOK

The text of *When Your Child Needs You* was set in Janson by ComCom, a division of the Haddon Craftsmen of Allentown, Pennsylvania. The book was printed and bound by R.R. Donnelley, Harrisonburg, Virginia division. The typography and binding were designed by Tom Suzuki of Falls Church, Virginia.